FRESH MOROCCAN

NADA SALEH

hamlyn

Note

The Food and Drug Administration advises that eggs should not be consumed raw. This book contains dishes made with raw or lightly cooked eggs. It is prudent for vulnerable people such as pregnant and nursing mothers, those with compromised immune systems, the elderly, babies, and young children to avoid uncooked or lightly cooked dishes made with eggs. Once prepared, these dishes should be kept refrigerated and used promptly.

This book includes dishes made with nuts and nut derivatives. It is advisable for customers with known allergic reactions to nuts and nut derivatives and those who may be potentially vulnerable to these allergies, such as pregnant and nursing mothers, those with compromised immune systems, the elderly, babies, and children to avoid dishes made with nuts and nut oils. It is also prudent to check the labels of pre-packaged ingredients for the possible inclusion of nut derivatives.

Ovens should be preheated to the specified temperature—if using a convection oven, follow the manufacturer's instructions for adjusting the time and the temperature.

First published in Great Britain in 2006 by
Hamlyn, a division of Octopus Publishing Group Ltd
2–4 Heron Quays, London E14 4JP

Contents

Introduction

My journey around Morocco started in the ancient city of Marrakech, founded in 1062 and an important crossroads for caravans as well as a meeting place for traders. At the famous Jemaa el-Fna market, where clouds of smoke rose from restaurant stalls busy grilling *kefta* and *merguez*, I saw storytellers, a snake charmer, a woman fortune-teller, and young men—made-up and dressed in women's clothing—belly dancing. A visit to the *souk*, a network of alleyways, revealed many souks within souks, but the one that fascinated me most of all sold fruits, vegetables, pyramids of colorful spices, buckets of purple, green, and black olives, and lemon and pepper confits. I saw heaps of pomegranates, introduced by the Phoenicians, who came to Morocco during their voyages in the 4th and 5th centuries BC, and who also brought the olive tree. Oranges, lemons, figs, dates, eggplants, artichokes, apricots, saffron, and much more were later introduced by the Arabs.

To the west of Marrakech lies Essaouira, a fortified town on the Atlantic coast. Here I sampled delicious specialties such as Fish Tagine with Couscous, cooked with onions and raisins (*see page 112*) and Sardines in Aromatic Herbs—balls of minced sardine in tomato sauce (*see page 106*). Farther down the coast is Agadir, famous for its sardine fisheries, while inland to the east is the village of Sidi al Mukhtar, which produces cumin, much used in Moroccan cuisine, and Tarazout, where bananas are grown.

In the Atlas mountains, the people of a Berber village greeted me and with great generosity prepared the specialties of the region, such as *Urkimen* (couscous of barley semolina, *see page 120*), *Amlou* (*see page 11*), and many others, to which each family contributed. One brought the onions, another the corn, some the almonds and the honey, and so on.

Among the rocks and hills of the Atlas mountains, cactuses abound, and the prickly pear fruit (barbary fig) can be found. The thorns are removed using palm leaves, then the skin is peeled and the fruit is dried in the sun to use in winter, in some regions in couscous. In summer when the prickly pear is ripe, sellers slice open the fruit, which are orangey in color and very tasty. The mountain evenings are cool, and I welcomed the nourishing Berber tagines of meat, carrots, potatoes, peas, and olives, such as the one I enjoyed at Tafraout. My first trip to Morocco years ago was to Fez, one of the holiest places in Morocco. I was then, as I still am today, overwhelmed by its mysterious and magical appeal. The market, a labyrinth of narrow alleyways, is a magnet to shoppers and a feast for the senses. Aromas of wild herbs and spices mingle with street food, while the sight of fruits and vegetables makes you dream of the filo pie *B'steeya* (*see page 72*) for which Fez is famous, delicious tagines such as *Maqfoul*, lamb with tomatoes and onions (*see page 95*), and the fig and walnut dishes of the south, or the apricot and almond dishes of the north.

Many dynasties have ruled Morocco, and many diverse influences are reflected in her culture and way of life. Moroccan cuisine seems to be distinct from that of the Middle Eastern and the other North African cuisines, as if to make a statement of independence and pride. Independence, because the Ottomans stopped their expansion more or less on the kingdom's borders, and pride, because Morocco was the springboard and the main source of manpower for the invasion and occupation of Spain from the 8th century AD onwards. A prestigious past and a population of Berbers, Arabs, and Jews have left their mark on present-day cuisine. Many dishes that appear in ancient Arab literature are evidence of that influence.

Sharing regular meals is an important factor in the life of Moroccans, and home cooking is a natural part of everyday life—it's a joy for everyone and brings the family together. Throughout this book you will find wholesome recipes that promote health and longevity. They are low in fat and in salt and are therefore a good choice for those who wish to lose excess weight.

NADA SALEH

Healthy eating

We live at a time when there is much controversy about what we eat. One day we are told how beneficial a foodstuff is, while the next we are advised to avoid it. Should we use butter, or is it high in saturated fats? Would it be better to follow the high-protein Atkins diet, or should we become vegetarians? How can we tell what is best, and how can we look after our health?

A balanced diet

In my early teens my first concern was to stay slim at any cost. I could have avoided my repeated diets and resulting weight gain if I had just eaten the nutritious home-cooked meals that my mother provided. I deprived myself of the foods and fats essential for building the immune system and providing the vital fuel for achieving high levels of mental and emotional balance. I took this risk until I learned how important these foods are for our physical and mental well-being. Now my eating plan is backed by scientific research, logic, common sense, and the wisdom of our forebears.

Cooking wholesome dishes preserves one's health and vitality, and they don't necessarily require expensive ingredients. Stock up with beans, chickpeas, lentils, peas, couscous, rice, spices, olive oil, nuts and seeds, and so on—all valuable sources of vegetable protein, vitamins, and minerals. Serve them with fresh vegetables to produce delicious meals for your family and friends. With home cooking, you know what's on your plate since you're in control of the quality and quantity of the ingredients.

Sweet treats

Life can have cruel moments, and sometimes we find ourselves reaching for fatty and sugary foods that provide temporary comfort. Occasionally this is acceptable, although the need for rapid gratification should be satisfied by nutrient-rich food that helps the brain to handle the stresses of life. Make snacks such as briouats (see pages 136–141), milk puddings, soups, and salads so that when you open the refrigerator you will always find something nourishing and satisfying to eat.

Having treats for dessert is fine, too, but rather than indulging in high-fat, high-sugar choices, prepare dishes such as Rice Pudding with Almonds (*see page 148*) or Dried Fruit Salad (*see page 152*). By eating healthily, you can relax after a meal without feeling guilty about having eaten unnecessary calories. Or, if you wish to cut out desserts but still want to satisfy a sweet tooth, try tagines such as Lamb Tagine with Prunes and Apricots (*see page 78*) and Chicken, Chickpeas, and Raisins (*see page 68*).

Reducing fat in your diet

Nonetheless, fats are warming and good sources of energy; they cushion and protect body organs, keep brain and body cells healthy, calm the nerves, and are necessary for the assimilation of the fat-soluble vitamins A, D, E, and K. There are three types of fats: saturated fatty acids, found in meat, cheese, butter, egg yolk, cream, and palm oil; monounsaturated fatty acids, found in olive and nut oils, avocados, and olives; and polyunsaturated fatty acids, including the essential omega-3 and omega-6 fatty acids found in corn, argan, soybeans, safflower, and sunflower oils, sesame seeds, walnuts, oily fish, pumpkin, and evening primrose oil.

A lifetime commitment to good eating habits is vital for building immunity and mental alertness. Many studies of the diets of Mediterranean countries show that those who follow these diets have a low percentage of heart problems, high blood pressure, cancers, and memory loss. These findings show that you should eat a varied diet and cut back on saturated fats, as those are increasingly linked to cardiovascular problems, many cancers, obesity, high levels of bad (LDL) cholesterol, and much more.

I have therefore sought out cuisines with dishes high in nutritional value but low in saturated fats such as butter. Moroccan food fits these criteria. It delivers a substantial variety of dishes with intriguing mixtures of ingredients, with plenty of flavor and an abundance of nutrients to satisfy bodily needs. For example, the famous *B'steeya (see page 72)* is a rich mixture of chicken or pigeon, herbs, spices, eggs, and almonds enveloped in layers of *warka* (filo pastry). Cutting down on the butter that's normally lavished over the pastry makes it easier to digest.

Complex carbohydrate dishes are another example. They are an excellent source of vegetable protein, protect the body, and help counteract insomnia and stress. They include dishes such as Barley Semolina Soup *(see page 24)*, or *Bissara (see page 26)*, a soup made from dried beans, garlic, spices, and cold-pressed olive oil, which calms the nerves and strengthens the immune system. Another warming soup is *Harira (see page 22)*; during the month of Ramadan, the fast is broken with *Harira* served with dates and

briouats, supplying the body with the building blocks of protein, vitamins, minerals, and energy. Fish dishes are also excellent—shrimp *(see page 108)* or sardines are a good source of omega-3 fatty acids, an essential oil that feeds brain cells, reduces bad (LDL) cholesterol and is anti-aging.

Moroccan food has many health-giving properties. For instance, onions and garlic help prevent blood clots and high blood pressure. Chicken, almonds, and dairy produce are a good source of protein and tryptophan, which is a natural remedy for insomnia. Herbs such as cilantro, parsley, mint, and thyme keep the circulation flowing, detoxify the body, and aid digestion.

Promoting good health Experiment with healthy ingredients, remembering at all times that the key to good health is balance, moderation, and positive thinking, combined with a sensible exercise and meditation routine. Too much of anything can have a detrimental effect on one's health.

Equipment

The utensils and equipment used in the Moroccan kitchen do not differ much from those in Western ones, except for the couscoussière.

ELECTRIC FOOD PROCESSOR, blender, or mixer to chop, mince, and purée vegetables, grains and legumes, fish, meat, or chicken.

PANS A selection of heavy-based skillets, casseroles, and nonstick pans in different sizes. Do not use aluminum pans—the metal leaches into the food.

COUSCOUSSIERE—a double pan. Stews and flavored stocks are cooked in the lower part, while the perforated upper part is used to steam couscous, vegetables, fish, and meat.

MORTAR AND PESTLE These are useful for creaming garlic or herbs and grinding spices and mastic (gum arabic). I like wooden ones as I find that the slightly rough interior surface aids the creaming or crushing. Remember to sprinkle a little salt over garlic and herbs, and sugar over mastic, before crushing. Always pound gently and rub against the mortar base.

STRAINERS AND COLANDERS in different sizes are useful for skimming, draining, and straining.

WOODEN SPOONS in various sizes. These are strong, practical, lightweight, and heat-resistant.

KNIVES One good knife to chop herbs, vegetables, and fruits and another for meat, fish, and chicken. Use a sharpening steel to keep knives sharp.

ADDITIONAL EQUIPMENT Spatulas, scissors, scales, measuring cups and spoons, and glass food containers are always useful.

Ingredients

ARGAN OIL This comes from the fruit of the argan tree (*Argan spinosa*), which grows in southwestern Morocco. It is rich in vitamin E and polyunsaturated fatty acids and has a strong flavor of hazelnut combined with a faint taste of ripe cheese.

Argan oil is used in salads and is delicious with couscous or sweet peppers, or sprinkled on cooked dishes. It is also used to make *Amlou*, a Berber delicacy in which finely chopped toasted almonds are kneaded to a smooth shiny consistency with argan oil and honey. This butter is highly prized. The best argan oil is cold-pressed; always buy it from a reputable store.

CINNAMON There are two types of cinnamon. True cinnamon is the inner bark from the tropical evergreen cinnamon tree dried and curled to form quills. It is light brown with a smooth surface and a sweetish flavor. It is widely available and mostly used in sweet dishes. The second type is the less expensive cassia, from the same family. Cassia bark is dark brown and thick with a rough texture and strong yet subtle flavor. Cassia bark and ground cassia are extensively used in Middle Eastern and North African cuisines, in savory dishes and sweets. Both cinnamon and cassia are used in *Ras al-hanout* (*see page 14*).

CLARIFIED BUTTER This is butter from which the milk solids have been removed. Because of this, it is purer than normal butter and can be heated to much higher temperatures. It will keep, refrigerated, for months. To prepare, see page 14.

COUSCOUS Couscous is the staple food of North Africa and is used in many savory and sweet dishes. It is made from hard wheat moistened with lightly salted water and a little flour. It is then rolled and strained into fine, medium, or large (coarse) pellets and traditionally dried in the sun, although today couscous is mostly sold ready-made. Couscous is steamed over the aromatic stew that accompanies it.

Barley couscous, *belboula*, is made from cracked or crushed barley or barley grits and is the traditional couscous of the Berbers in the south of Morocco. It is used in soups and in many couscous dishes, such as *Urkimen (see page 120)*. *Belboula* is sold in Moroccan stores in its raw state or precooked.

Corn couscous is generally eaten with Fish Tagine with Couscous (*see page 112*). *Beddaz*, a specialty of the region of Ourzazate, is a corn couscous dish in which the leaves of turnips are boiled until tender, drained, thinly sliced, and placed over the couscous grains.

In Morocco, couscous is eaten by forming a little of it into a ball, using three fingers of the right hand, and then conveying it to the mouth.

CUBEB CITRONELLE The berries of a climbing shrub, cubeb have a pungent, spicy flavor, and some have a hint of lemon. This spice is very much appreciated in Morocco and is used in the mixture of spices for *Ras al-hanout* (*see page 14*).

FRUCTOSE OR FRUIT SUGAR Fructose comes from honey and from fruit; it is sweeter and lower in calories than table sugar, so less is needed. Add it toward the end of cooking time; depending on the brand, fructose may become bitter if it simmers for a long time. Pure fructose sugar is available in health food stores—make sure you buy a good brand.

FRUIT OF THE ASH TREE (*FRAXINUS*) The fruit has silver-gray bark and feather-like foliage. Its clustered winged seeds are known in Morocco as *Lissanel-tair* (the tongue of the bird). It is included in the mixture of spices for *Ras al-hanout (see page 14)*.

GRAINS OF PARADISE (*AFRAMOMUM MELEGUETTA, MANIGUETTE*) This pungent, peppery spice originates from West Africa and is related to the ginger family. It is used in *Ras al-hanout (see page 14)*.

LONG PEPPER (*PIPER LONGUM*) This spice originated in southern Asia. It has a strong flavor similar to black pepper and is included in the mixture for *Ras al-hanout (see page 14)*.

MALLOW (*MALVA SYLVESTRIS*) This prolific plant originated from the Mediterranean region, but now grows throughout the world. In Morocco, where it is very much appreciated, it is known as *Bekkoula* and the leaves are used in savory dishes.

MASTIC (GUM ARABIC) A resin from the trunk of the *Pistacia lentiscus* tree, native to the eastern Mediterranean. In Morocco it is used to flavor milk puddings and in *Ras al-hanout (see page 14)*. Only a small amount is needed to add its unique flavor.

MINT Several varieties grow in abundance in Morocco and it is widely used to flavor salads and also added to bread and cakes, especially in the eastern and northern parts of Morocco. It is also, of course, made into mint tea. Mint goes beautifully with tomatoes, eggplants, beets, and carrots; it flavors yogurt and cucumber salad, and is ideal with fresh or dried fruit salads and watermelon.

ORANGE FLOWER WATER This is the essence distilled from the blossoms of the Seville orange, *Citrus aurantium*. It is very fragrant and in Morocco is used in abundance in salads, tagines, and in sweets. It is also added to the water used for washing hands before and after eating.

POMEGRANATE SYRUP This is made by boiling the juice from pomegranate seeds until it becomes a relatively thick syrup. It can be made with sweet or sour pomegranates. The sour syrup is generally used to complement the flavor of certain vegetables, particularly eggplants, meat dishes such as Shreds of Lamb in Pomegranate Juice (*see page 94*), and some salads. The sweet syrup is used in drinks.

ROSEWATER This is a fragrant essence distilled from the damask rose, *Rosa damascena*. Rosewater is used extensively in sweets and sweet pastries, as well as some rice dishes; in many parts of Morocco rose buds are added to the mixture of *Ras al-hanout (see page 14)*.

Basic recipes

Harissa

This Tunisian chili paste is much appreciated in Morocco. I prepare it using sweet red peppers and mild chilies as well as hot chilies, rather than just with hot chilies as they do in Tunisia. It's so

delicious that I spread it on olive bread to eat as a snack. Serve Harissa with potatoes, couscous, olives, anchovies, sardines, and grilled eggplants.

INGREDIENTS *2 red bell peppers, cored, seeded, and sliced* ‖ *1–2 mild red chilies, halved and seeded* ‖ *1 hot chili, seeded (optional)* ‖ *2 large garlic cloves* ‖ *pinch salt* ‖ *extra virgin olive oil*

ONE Put the red bell peppers and mild chili in the sun to dry. Depending on the strength of the sun, this might take 1–2 days. Alternatively, dry the bell peppers in a preheated oven, 300°F, for 15–20 minutes, then reduce heat to, 275°F, and roast for 30–40 minutes. Remove from oven and let to cool. Do the same with the mild chili, but be careful, because it dries out very quickly—within 5 minutes or less. **TWO** Place the bell peppers and mild chilies in a glass jar with the hot chili (if using), garlic, and salt; cover with oil. Seal the jar and leave for 3–4 days. **THREE** Transfer the contents of the jar to a food processor and blend until smooth. Return the purée to the jar and use as needed.

Makes about 1 cup

NUTRIENT ANALYSIS PER JAR 290 cal – 1200 kJ – 4 g protein – 16 g carbohydrate – 12 g sugars – 23 g fat – 3 g saturates – 4 g fiber – 0.01 g sodium (if no salt is added)

Preserved lemon

This is very simple to prepare. In Morocco, only the rind is used, in dishes such as *Tangia*, *Beqqoula*, Tagine of Chicken and Olives, and so on. The rind is cut into ¼ inch widths and the pulp is discarded. Rinse the preserved lemon before use.

INGREDIENTS *8 small unwaxed lemons (navel lemons, if possible)* ‖ *5 teaspoons sea salt, divided* ‖ *juice of 1 large lemon*

ONE Scrub the lemons under running water, then soak in cold water for 1 hour. Rinse and dry well with paper towels. **TWO** Cut each lemon into quarters lengthwise, from the point to about three-quarters of the way down, leaving them joined at the base. **THREE** Using a long-handled teaspoon, stuff the center of each lemon with ½ teaspoon of the salt, then pinch the sides together. Arrange the lemons upright, packed tightly together, in a sterilized jar. Shake in the remaining salt and the lemon juice, then place a weight on top (such as pie weights tied in cheesecloth). Alternatively, cover the lemons with warm water. **FOUR** Seal the jar and store in a dry dark place for 3–4 weeks before using.

Makes about 32 oz

NUTRIENT ANALYSIS PER JAR 144 cal – 600 kJ – 8 g protein – 25 g carbohydrate – 25 g sugars – 2 g fat – 1 g saturates – 34 g fiber – 9.9 g sodium

Ras al-hanout (Head of the Shop)

This is a famous Moroccan spice mix.

INGREDIENTS *1 tablespoon dried ginger* ‖ *¼ oz long pepper* ‖ *1 cinnamon stick* ‖ *¼ oz cassia bark* ‖ *¼ oz whole nutmeg* ‖ *3 star anise* ‖ *½ tablespoon cardamom seeds* ‖ *½ tablespoon white peppercorns* ‖ *½ tablespoon juniper berries* ‖ *7 cloves* ‖ *7–10 small pieces mastic (gum arabic)* ‖ *½ tablespoon cubeb citronelle* ‖ *½ tablespoon ground mace* ‖ *½ tablespoon grains of paradise (maniguette)* ‖ *½ tablespoon fruit of the ash tree* ‖ *1 tablespoon turmeric* ‖ *½ tablespoon galangal*

ONE Blend all ingredients to a powder in a coffee or spice grinder.

Makes about 2 oz

NUTRIENT ANALYSIS PER JAR 70 cal – 290 kJ – 4 g protein – 13 g carbohydrate – 3 g sugars – 5 g fat – 2 g saturates – 0 g fiber – 0.01 g sodium

Chermoula sauce

INGREDIENTS *¼ cup ground coriander* ‖ *2 garlic cloves, peeled* ‖ *1 teaspoon salt* ‖ *2 teaspoons ground cumin* ‖ *1 teaspoon paprika* ‖ *¼ teaspoon cayenne pepper* ‖ *½ teaspoon turmeric* ‖ *1 tablespoon lemon juice* ‖ *1 tablespoon extra virgin olive oil* ‖ *1 ice cube*

ONE Blend all ingredients in a food processor until smooth.

Makes about 3½ oz

NUTRIENT ANALYSIS FOR TOTAL 324 cal – 1349 kJ – 10 g protein – 21 g carbohydrate – 0 g sugars – 24 g fat – 2 g saturates – 0 g fiber – 2.0 g sodium

Clarified butter

INGREDIENTS *2 sticks (1 cup) butter*

ONE Put butter in a pan and place over a medium heat for 1–2 minutes until it melts and starts to bubble. **TWO** Remove pan from heat and skim the froth from the surface. **THREE** Carefully pour the clear butter into a bowl, leaving the milk solids in the pan.

Makes 2–3 cups

NUTRIENT ANALYSIS FOR WHOLE AMOUNT 1658 cal – 6820 kJ – 0 g protein – 0 g carbohydrate – 0 g sugars – 184 g fat – 122 g saturates – 0 g fiber – 0.8 g sodium (for salted butter), 0 g sodium (for unsalted butter)

How to prepare couscous

To cook couscous the traditional way (using uncooked couscous, not the precooked variety that is commonly sold), the grains are rinsed and drained, then spread over a large wooden tray or shallow pan and aerated, using the fingers in a circular motion. The grains are then left for 15–30 minutes until the water is fully absorbed and the grains are relatively dry. Then the grains are gently rubbed between the palms to break down any lumps. Next, they are transferred to the perforated top section of the couscoussière, placed over the lower part, which is filled two-thirds full with boiling water or a stew, and left to steam. While steaming the grains, do not cover them with a lid, otherwise they will become soggy. The steam from the lower part enters through the holes to cook the grains.

When steam escapes through the grains, remove and spread over the tray or pan. The grains are moistened with 3–4 handfuls of water and, as before, they are aerated and left until the water is absorbed, this time for 10–15 minutes. They are then rubbed again to break down any lumps, transferred for a second time to the couscoussière and steamed for about 15–20 minutes. The grains are removed and spread over the tray or pan. At this stage salt is sprinkled on. Repeat the whole process one more time, then spread the grains over a serving dish and mix in oil or butter, using the back of a wooden spoon to gently break down any lumps. Depending on the recipe, stock, honey, or milk may be added at this stage. The cooked couscous is piled into a pyramid shape and served with whatever the recipe calls for—dates, raisins, vegetables, meat, chicken, or fish.

If you do not have a couscoussière, place the couscous grains in a fine-mesh strainer and rest it over boiling water or a stew, then cook as above. Make sure that the strainer is high enough out of the water so that only steam reaches the grains, not the water.

Barley couscous is steamed twice, each time for 30 minutes, following the preparation above. Nowadays, many varieties of vegetables or dried fruit are invariably added to couscous. I was told that the finest dishes of couscous with fruits were prepared by the Jewish Fassiates (of Fez). So let your imagination flow and experiment with couscous.

Mint tea

Coffee was very popular in Morocco until the English introduced tea, which is said to have been brought in through Gibraltar. Today tea is very popular and at every occasion, formal or not, tea infused with mint is offered as a form of greeting and is an accompaniment to the relaxing moments of the day. In the midst of Moroccan souks (markets) and rural streets, silver or copper trays carrying glasses filled with mint tea sweetened with many lumps of sugar are passed around from stalls and in cafés to soothe dry mouths.

Mint tea has become Morocco's national drink, but there are also numerous local tea preparations flavored with scented herbs or spices, depending on the region. The Moroccans use green tea, to which is added absinthe (wormwood), saffron, mint, orange tree blossoms, cloves, and, in winter, *Ras al-hanout* (*see page 14*), which gives warmth.

Green tea is highly beneficial—its caffeine is negligible and does not affect the nervous system, it raises the metabolism, keeps fat burning, and is rich in substances that may prevent the growth of cancer cells.

To make a cup of green tea, place ¾–1 teaspoon of green tea leaves (or to your liking, whether strong or weak) in a cup. Boil water, but wait 3 minutes before pouring it over the leaves. Once the water is added, infuse the leaves for 1–5 minutes. To add more fragrance, put a few fresh mint leaves, or any other herb or spice mentioned above, into the cup. The tea is best drunk without adding sugar.

Fish soup

This fish soup has wonderful aromas from the colorful variety of vegetables and spices, and tastes great the following day. Any other white fish, shrimp, or salmon can be used.

INGREDIENTS ½ tablespoon extra virgin olive oil ‖ 1 medium onion, finely chopped ‖ 4 garlic cloves, chopped ‖ good pinch saffron threads ‖ 2 tomatoes, chopped ‖ 1 teaspoon salt, divided or to taste ‖ 7½ cups water, divided ‖ 2 lb sea bass with head, scaled and gutted ‖ ½ teaspoon ground black pepper ‖ pinch nutmeg ‖ bouquet garni: 2 bay leaves, ½ lemon, a few black peppercorns, 5 parsley sprigs, tied in a cheesecloth ‖ 1 medium stalk celery, finely diced ‖ ½ bulb fennel, coarsely grated ‖ 2 carrots, coarsely grated ‖ ½–¾ teaspoon turmeric ‖ handful finely chopped cilantro leaves

ONE Heat oil in a medium pan; sauté the onions and garlic for 1–2 minutes. Crumble in the saffron and stir; add the tomatoes and ½ teaspoon of the salt and simmer over low heat for 2–3 minutes. Add 2½ cups of the water and bring to a boil; reduce heat and simmer for 10–15 minutes. **TWO** Transfer mixture to a blender or food processor and blend until smooth. **THREE** Rinse the fish and pat dry, then rub inside and out with the remaining salt; sprinkle the cavity with a pinch of the pepper and the nutmeg. Remove the fish head. Slice the fish into 3 pieces. **FOUR** Put the bouquet garni in a large pan with the fish head and pieces on top. Add the remaining water and place over medium heat, skimming off any scum with a slotted spoon. Add the tomato mixture and bring to a boil. Add the celery, fennel, and carrots, reduce heat, and cook gently for 5 minutes or until the fish is cooked. Transfer the fish pieces to a plate. **FIVE** Simmer the vegetables and fish head for another 8–10 minutes, then remove and discard the fish head; add the remaining pepper, the turmeric, and cilantro. Bone the fish, discard bones, and return the fish to the stock; simmer gently, 1 minute. Remove the bouquet garni. Squeeze in the juice from the lemon. Serve the soup hot with bread and olives.

Serves 4–6

NUTRIENT ANALYSIS PER SERVING 235 cal – 986 kJ – 38 g protein – 7 g carbohydrate – 6 g sugars – 7 g fat – 1 g saturates – 2 g fiber – 0.6 g sodium (if using 1 teaspoon salt)

HEALTHY TIP This dish is low in fat with valuable amounts of anti-stress B vitamins, potassium, magnesium, phosphorus, and sulfur, and also betacarotene and lycopene, which guard against various cancers.

Pumpkin soup

Here is a delicious, colorful soup inspired by a meaty pumpkin soup that Jewish people in Marrakech prepare for their Passover feast.

INGREDIENTS: *2¼ lb peeled pumpkin, seeded and cut into chunks ‖ 8 oz sweet potato, cut into chunks ‖ 5 cups water ‖ 1 onion, halved ‖ 1 cinnamon stick ‖ 2 large garlic cloves ‖ 2 teaspoons salt, or to taste ‖ 3 tablespoons extra virgin olive oil ‖ ½ cup dried chickpeas, soaked, drained, and precooked (see page 20) ‖ large handful of fresh or frozen fava beans, skinned ‖ 1 teaspoon turmeric ‖ good pinch black pepper ‖ 4–5 tablespoons thick plain yogurt with active cultures ‖ large handful finely chopped parsley or mint*

ONE Put the pumpkin and sweet potato in a pan and add the water, onion, cinnamon stick, garlic, salt, and ½ tablespoon of the oil. Bring to a boil, reduce heat to medium-low, and simmer for 10–15 minutes until tender. **TWO** Remove and discard the cinnamon stick. Transfer the mixture to a blender or food processor and blend until smooth (you may have to do this in 2 batches), or press through a strainer. Pour the soup back into the pan, add the chickpeas (if desired, skin before adding) and fava beans, and simmer over medium-low heat. **THREE** Put 1½ tablespoons of the remaining oil, the turmeric, and pepper in a small bowl, add the yogurt, and stir until smooth. Stir this into the pumpkin mixture and mix well, then let simmer for 5–7 minutes, stirring occasionally. **FOUR** Meanwhile, heat a small skillet, add the remaining oil and the parsley, stir for a few seconds, and remove from heat. (If using mint, do not sauté; just mix into the hot oil.) **FIVE** To serve, pour the soup into a large bowl and stir in the parsley or mint. Alternatively, pour into individual bowls and add 1 tablespoon of the parsley or mint to each. Eat with a good crusty bread.

Serves 4

NUTRIENT ANALYSIS PER SERVING 310 cal – 1299 kJ – 12 g protein – 35 g carbohydrate – 13 g sugars – 15 g fat – 4 g saturates – 7 g fiber – 1 g sodium (if using 2 teaspoons salt)

HEALTHY TIP This soup is rich in ingredients containing compounds that are anti-cancer and anti-aging; it is also high in antioxidants, betacarotene, and the B and E vitamins.

Vegetarian harira soup

The zucchini, pumpkin, and fresh ginger make this a wholesome dish, and since it is free of animal meat and fat, it is also light on the stomach and the pocket.

INGREDIENTS *¼ cup dried chickpeas, soaked overnight* ‖ *6–7½ cups water* ‖ *¼ cup brown lentils* ‖ *¼ cup brown basmati rice, rinsed once and drained* ‖ *2 tablespoons split dried fava beans, soaked 10 minutes and drained* ‖ *1 onion, finely chopped* ‖ *2 medium stalks celery, with leaves if possible, finely diced* ‖ *1 zucchini, finely diced* ‖ *1 carrot, finely diced* ‖ *6 oz peeled pumpkin, seeded and finely diced* ‖ *2 tablespoons extra virgin olive oil, divided* ‖ *pinch saffron threads* ‖ *1 teaspoon turmeric* ‖ *2 teaspoons tomato paste* ‖ *1 lb tomatoes, peeled, seeded, and finely diced* ‖ *1 tablespoon all-purpose flour* ‖ *2 large handfuls finely chopped cilantro leaves* ‖ *2 large handfuls finely chopped parsley, plus extra sprigs for garnish* ‖ *1½ teaspoons salt, or to taste* ‖ *good pinch black pepper* ‖ *about ½ teaspoon freshly grated ginger root* ‖ *lemon juice (optional)* ‖ *2–4 lemon wedges*

ONE Drain the chickpeas and rinse well, then put in a large pan with the water. Bring slowly to a boil, skimming the surface as foam forms; reduce heat to low, cover, and simmer for 1½–2 hours or until very soft. **TWO** Add the lentils, cover, and simmer for 10 minutes. Add the rice, fava beans, onion, celery, zucchini, carrot, and pumpkin; cover and simmer for 20 minutes. **THREE** Meanwhile, heat 1 tablespoon of the oil in a medium pan, add the saffron, a pinch of the turmeric, and the tomato paste, and stir. Add the tomatoes, breaking them up with the back of a wooden spoon, and simmer for 1–2 minutes before adding to the soup. Bring to a boil; reduce heat to low, cover, and simmer for 15–20 minutes. **FOUR** About 5 minutes before the end of cooking time, ladle 1–2 tablespoons of the soup stock into a bowl and stir in the flour until smooth. Stir this into the soup, adding the remaining oil, the cilantro, and parsley, then season with the salt, remaining turmeric, the pepper, and ginger. **FIVE** Taste and adjust the seasonings. Serve hot, sprinkled with a little lemon juice, if using, with the lemon wedges, garnished with parsley sprigs.

Serves 4–6

NUTRIENT ANALYSIS PER SERVING 267 cal – 1126 kJ – 11 g protein – 40 g carbohydrate – 10 g sugars – 8 g fat – 1 g saturates – 6 g fiber – 0.8 g sodium (if using 1½ teaspoons salt)

HEALTHY TIP

This soup is a gold mine of nutrients and protein that strengthen the immune system, give a glow to the skin, feed the nervous system, and are excellent for premenopausal women. The soup detoxes the whole body.

Harira

During Ramadan, at the setting of the sun the fast is broken with Harira. It is traditionally served with lemon wedges, dates, and *Chebakia* (honeyed cakes), but could be served as a one-pot meal, followed by some fresh fruit.

INGREDIENTS *½ cup dried chickpeas, soaked overnight ‖ 7½ cups water, divided ‖ 1½ tablespoons extra virgin olive oil, divided ‖ 9 oz lamb (leg, shoulder, or neck), finely diced ‖ 1 cinnamon stick ‖ 1 bay leaf ‖ ⅓ cup brown lentils ‖ ⅓ cup split dried fava beans, soaked for 10 minutes and drained ‖ 1 lb tomatoes ‖ 2 medium onions, finely chopped ‖ 4 large stalks celery, finely chopped ‖ 2½ oz cilantro leaves, finely chopped ‖ 2½ oz parsley, finely chopped ‖ 1 teaspoon turmeric ‖ ½ tablespoon black pepper ‖ ½ teaspoon saffron threads ‖ ½ teaspoon ground ginger ‖ 1½ teaspoons salt, or to taste ‖ 1 heaping teaspoon tomato paste ‖ 2 tablespoons brown rice ‖ 2 tablespoons all-purpose flour ‖ lemon juice (optional)*

ONE Drain the chickpeas and rinse well. Put in a large pan with 5 cups of the water and bring slowly to a boil, skimming the surface as foam forms. Reduce heat, cover, and simmer for 1 hour. **TWO** Meanwhile, heat ¼ tablespoon of the oil in a skillet and sauté the lamb for 1–2 minutes. Add to the chickpeas with the cinnamon stick, bay leaf, lentils, and fava beans and bring to a boil. Reduce heat, cover, and simmer for another 30 minutes. **THREE** Meanwhile, purée the tomatoes in a food processor until smooth. **FOUR** Heat the remaining oil in a medium pan and sauté the onions for 2–3 minutes; add the celery and sauté for 2 minutes until translucent, but do not brown. Stir in the cilantro, parsley, turmeric, pepper, saffron, ginger, salt, and tomato paste and stir well. Add the puréed tomatoes and 2 cups of the remaining water. Pour this mixture into the chickpeas and lamb, add the rice, and bring to a boil. Reduce heat, cover, and simmer for 30 minutes. **FIVE** Meanwhile, place the flour in a bowl and add the remaining water, whisking continuously. About 15 minutes before the end of cooking time, stir the mixture into the chickpeas and lamb and keep stirring until it boils; reduce heat and simmer for the remainder of the cooking time. **SIX** Taste and adjust the seasonings. Serve hot, sprinkled with a little lemon juice, if using.

Serves 4–6

NUTRIENT ANALYSIS PER SERVING 453 cal – 1908 kJ – 32 g protein – 52 g carbohydrate – 10 g sugars – 15 g fat – 4 g saturates – 9 g fiber – 0.9 g sodium (if using 1½ teaspoons salt)

HEALTHY TIP Harira is rich in protein, an important immunity builder, and also in fiber. It is excellent for diabetics and helps to prevent diabetes, since its sugars are released very slowly into the bloodstream.

Puréed chickpea soup

I love the thick purée of chickpeas you find in Morocco, and here I have added a little more water to produce a soothing and nourishing soup. It is simple and quick to prepare. Authentically, the chickpeas are skinned, which is not difficult to do, but keeping the skins on saves time and increases their fiber content.

INGREDIENTS *1¼ cups dried chickpeas, soaked overnight, or 15 oz canned chickpeas, drained and rinsed ‖ 6 cups water ‖ 1 garlic clove ‖ 1 small–medium onion, chopped ‖ ½ teaspoon saffron threads ‖ 1 tablespoon butter or extra virgin olive oil ‖ ½ teaspoon ground or freshly grated ginger root ‖ 1 teaspoon salt, or to taste ‖ lemon wedges (optional)*

ONE Drain the chickpeas and rinse well. Put in a pan with the water and bring slowly to a boil, skimming the surface as foam forms. Reduce heat, cover, and simmer for 2 hours or until soft. If using canned chickpeas, bring the water to a boil, then add the chickpeas with the ingredients at step two. **TWO** Add the garlic, onion, saffron, and butter or oil and bring to a boil; reduce heat, cover, and simmer for 30–40 minutes. **THREE** Remove from heat and stir in the ginger and salt. Transfer the mixture to a blender or food processor and purée until smooth, or press through a fine-mesh strainer. Serve hot, with the lemon wedges, if using, and eat with whole grain croutons.

Serves 4–6

NUTRIENT ANALYSIS PER SERVING 35 cal – 990 kJ – 214 g protein – 33 g carbohydrate – 3 g sugars – 7 g fat – 2 g saturates – 9 g fiber – 0.5 g sodium

HEALTHY TIP Chickpeas are a wonderful fuel for the body. Naturally rich in protective compounds and phytonutrients, they are also high in protein, B vitamins, and iron. Eating chickpeas on a regular basis benefits the nerves, the heart, good (HDL) cholesterol, and menopausal women.

Barley semolina soup

During my stay in the Atlas Mountains, this soup (known as *Tchicha*) was prepared for me. It's thick and velvety like hot cereal and uses lots of thyme (excellent for the hair) and garlic.

INGREDIENTS *7½ cups water* ‖ *5 large garlic cloves* ‖ *1 teaspoon salt, divided or to taste* ‖ *1¼ cups barley semolina* ‖ *1¼ cups 2 percent milk* ‖ *2–3 heaping tablespoons thyme leaves* ‖ *3 tablespoons extra virgin olive oil* ‖ *½ teaspoon black pepper*

ONE Place the water and garlic in a large pan and bring to a boil; reduce heat to medium-low. Cook for 1 minute, then transfer the garlic to a plate, discard the skin, add ½ teaspoon of the salt, and crush until creamy. Stir this into the pan with the barley semolina and simmer, stirring occasionally, until it boils and reaches a thick consistency. **TWO** Gradually stir in the milk and bring to a boil; reduce heat and simmer for 8–10 minutes, stirring occasionally. **THREE** Meanwhile, gently crush the thyme with a little of the remaining salt in a mortar with a pestle. Heat a small skillet, add the oil, turn off the heat, and stir in the thyme—it should sizzle. This should be done quickly without burning the thyme. **FOUR** Sprinkle the soup with the pepper, then taste and adjust the salt. Stir the oil and thyme into the soup and serve; alternatively, serve the soup in individual bowls and drizzle some oil and thyme over each.

Serves 6

NUTRIENT ANALYSIS PER SERVING 226 cal – 957 kJ – 5 g protein – 38 g carbohydrate – 3 g sugars – 7 g fat – 1 g saturates – 3 g fiber – 0.4 g sodium (if using 1 teaspoon salt)

HEALTHY TIP This wholesome soup is rich in E and B vitamins, calcium, magnesium, manganese, selenium, sulfur, phosphorus, germanium, chromium, and silicon. It also uses lots of garlic, which, as well as adding flavor, lowers high blood pressure, strengthens brain cells, increases immunity, and protects the body from the ravages of free radicals. Garlic also acts as an antibiotic, calms the nerves, aids circulation, is good for hair and skin, and is said to be anti-aging and even an aphrodisiac!

Fava bean soup

Bissara is a famous purée of fava beans infused with garlic that is served with bread all over Morocco, especially for breakfast (although in Fez and Meknès, it is eaten at any time of the day). Here, I have added more water to turn it into a soup. It is an economical dish, as well as being substantial and strengthening. For vegetarians it is important to include other types of beans and/or nuts in order to provide extra protein. Serve with a tomato and onion salad or any other salad rich in vitamin C, which will aid the absorption of iron.

INGREDIENTS *1¼ cups split dried fava beans, soaked 10 minutes and drained ‖ 4–5 cups water ‖ 12 garlic cloves ‖ 1¾ teaspoons salt, or to taste ‖ 3 tablespoons extra virgin olive oil ‖ 1 teaspoon ground cumin ‖ 1 teaspoon paprika ‖ a little chopped mint (optional) ‖ chili pepper (optional)*

ONE Rinse the fava beans and place with the water in a large pan over medium heat. Bring slowly to a boil, skimming the surface as foam forms. Add the garlic; reduce heat to low, cover, and simmer for 15–20 minutes or until beans are soft. Sprinkle with the salt and remove from heat. **TWO** Transfer the mixture to a blender or food processor and purée until smooth and creamy (you may have to do this in batches), or rub through a fine-mesh strainer. Pour back into the pan and reheat for 1–2 minutes. **THREE** Meanwhile, mix the oil, cumin, and paprika together in a small bowl until smooth. **FOUR** Pour the soup into a large bowl or individual bowls and drizzle with the oil mixture and a pinch of mint and chili pepper, if using. Eat with a good whole grain bread or croutons.

Serves 4–6

NUTRIENT ANALYSIS PER SERVING 307 cal – 1280 kJ – 18 g protein – 37 g carbohydrate – 0 g sugars – 9 g fat – 1 g saturates – 8 g fiber – 0.8 g sodium (if using 1¾ teaspoons salt)

HEALTHY TIP This dish is very rich in E and B vitamins, iron, fiber, and sulfur and is excellent for diabetics or those with high blood pressure. Garlic is a powerful antibiotic, nerve calmer, rejuvenator, and is known as an aphrodisiac—substances in garlic stimulate the sex glands. The great physician Dioscorides praised it highly.

Salads

Couscous and mint salad

This is a traditional, simple salad made with a delicious mixture of aromatic herbs, spices, and tomatoes. Argan oil, rich in polyunsaturated and monounsaturated fats, gives the salad a lovely nutty flavor, and is good for the heart. If it is not available, olive oil is an excellent substitute, as it reduces cholesterol.

INGREDIENTS *1 cup organic couscous ‖ 2 tablespoons argan or extra virgin olive oil ‖ 1–1½ tablespoons dried mint ‖ 3 tomatoes, peeled, seeded, and finely diced ‖ 1 large garlic clove, crushed ‖ 1 onion or 4 small green onions, finely chopped ‖ 3 tablespoons lemon juice ‖ ¼ teaspoon cayenne pepper*

ONE Cover the couscous with water. Rake it through with your fingers, then drain and immediately spread it evenly over a large tray or shallow pan. Rake the grains with your fingers a few times to aerate them, then leave for 20–30 minutes until the water is absorbed and the couscous is relatively dry. **TWO** Rub the couscous gently between your palms, allowing it to fall back into the tray or pan, to break down any lumps. Repeat until the couscous has no lumps. **THREE** Rub your palms with a little of the oil and repeat the process. Alternatively, drizzle the oil over the couscous and rake through the grains. **FOUR** Add the mint, rub it in well, then add all the remaining ingredients, mixing gently yet thoroughly. Leave for 5 minutes to allow the flavors to come together, then serve.

Serves 4–6

NUTRIENT ANALYSIS PER SERVING 180 cal – 752 kJ – 4 g protein – 29 g carbohydrate – 2g sugars – 6 g fat – 1 g saturates – 1 g fiber – 0.007 g sodium

HEALTHY TIP This salad includes garlic and onion, both of which have powerful substances that stimulate enzymes responsible for eliminating toxins from our bodies. It is rich in antioxidants, which stabilize free radicals, thus protecting us from degenerative diseases.

Beet salad

Beet salad is one of many salads that usually precedes the indulgent main dishes of Morocco, such as a tagine. Beets are low in calories and are an excellent source of antioxidants as well as being rich in vitamin B9, potassium, and iron. Even their leaves hold a lot of nutrients.

INGREDIENTS *1 lb beets, with peels on* ‖ *1 garlic clove* ‖ *pinch salt, or to taste* ‖ *3–4 mint leaves* ‖ *1 heaping tablespoon cilantro, chopped* ‖ *½ tablespoon thyme* ‖ *1 teaspoon honey* ‖ *1 teaspoon fructose (fruit sugar)* ‖ *1 teaspoon extra virgin olive oil* ‖ *juice of ½ orange* ‖ *3 clementines, peeled and broken into segments* ‖ *¾–1 tablespoon orange flower water* ‖ *1 tablespoon parsley, finely chopped*

ONE Wash the beets and place in a steamer with a tight-fitting lid. Steam until tender, then remove and allow to cool. **TWO** Peel the beets and cut into small cubes. In a mortar, add the garlic, salt, mint, cilantro, and thyme. Pound with the pestle until it reaches a creamy consistency, then incorporate the honey, fructose (fruit sugar), oil, and orange juice. **THREE** Place the beets, clementine segments (do not remove their skin), flower water, and parsley into a serving bowl, drizzle with the dressing, then toss and serve.

Serves 4

NUTRIENT ANALYSIS PER SERVING 80 cal – 338 kJ – 11 g protein – 63 g carbohydrate – 59 g sugars – 1 g fat – 1 g saturates – 4 g fiber – 0.09 g sodium (if no salt is added)

HEALTHY TIP Health and pleasure go hand in hand in this therapeutic combination. It has protective qualities and helps combat degenerative diseases.

Lettuce and orange salad

Once you have tasted this salad, you'll be hooked. While I was assembling the lettuce and oranges, I was inspired to add some dates, honey, and walnuts, since it was fall—the season for walnuts. These ingredients are not foreign to the Moroccan kitchen and they enrich this salad, upgrading it to a dish fit for a festive lunch or dinner.

INGREDIENTS *8–10 Romaine lettuce leaves* ‖ *3 oranges* ‖ *4 medjool dates, cubed* ‖ *4–6 shelled walnuts, coarsely chopped* ‖ *½ teaspoon sea salt* ‖ *1 tablespoon extra virgin olive oil* ‖ *½ tablespoon honey* ‖ *½ tablespoon orange flower water* ‖ *½ tablespoon lemon juice* ‖ *a dash black pepper* ‖ *a few mint leaves, coarsely chopped*

ONE Slice the lettuce leaves into thin to medium ribbons. Peel 2½ of the oranges and cut into small to medium pieces. Squeeze the juice of the remaining ½ orange and add to a bowl with the lettuce leaves, oranges, dates, walnuts, salt, and oil. **TWO** Dissolve the honey in the flower water and lemon juice and add to the ingredients in the bowl. Sprinkle with the pepper and mint, toss thoroughly, and serve.

Serves 4

NUTRIENT ANALYSIS PER SERVING 187 cal – 787 kJ – 3 g protein – 25 g carbohydrate – 25 g sugars – 9 g fat – 1 g saturates – 4 g fiber – 0.3 g sodium

HEALTHY TIP This is an extremely refreshing and nutritious salad with valuable anticancer carotenoids such as vitamin C. It is rich in calcium, potassium, phosphates, iron, folic acid, silicon, fiber, and lutein. Remember to use the pith of the oranges; it is high in bioflavonoids, which are excellent for blood vessels. Another benefit is that substances in lettuce leaves induce sleep.

Aromatic carrot salad

Here is a refreshing and nutritious carrot salad. It makes a light appetizer to a meal or can be eaten as a snack, as a good alternative to sugary sweets.

INGREDIENTS *1 lb carrots, peeled and cut into rounds or sticks* ‖ *⅔ cup water* ‖ *1 teaspoon paprika* ‖ *½ teaspoon salt* ‖ *¾–1 teaspoon ground cumin* ‖ *½ teaspoon sugar* ‖ *1 tablespoon extra virgin olive oil* ‖ *½ tablespoon finely chopped cilantro leaves* ‖ *½ tablespoon cider vinegar* ‖ *½ tablespoon lemon juice* ‖ *1 teaspoon orange flower water (optional)*

ONE Put the carrots and water in a medium pan and bring to a boil; reduce heat to medium, cover, and simmer for 2–3 minutes or until the water has reduced to 1 tablespoon. **TWO** Stir in the paprika, salt, cumin, sugar, oil, cilantro, and vinegar. Stir for a few seconds, then remove from heat and stir in the lemon juice and flower water, if using. **THREE** Let cool, then serve—the flavor improves as it cools.

Serves 4

NUTRIENT ANALYSIS PER SERVING 72 cal – 297 kJ – 1 g protein – 11 g carbohydrate – 10 g sugars – 3 g fat – 1 g saturates – 3 g fiber – 0.3 g sodium

HEALTHY TIP This salad is rich in betacarotene, calcium, fiber, and E and C vitamins, both potent antioxidants that inhibit cancer formation. As well as adding flavor, cumin helps to relieve flatulence.

Grated carrot and orange salad

This is a delicious, refreshing, and nutritious salad, ideal to eat at any time of the day or on any occasion. I have added some pine nuts for extra flavor and have substituted honey for sugar, because honey is rich in mineral salts and its health-giving properties have been known since ancient times.

INGREDIENTS *1 tablespoon honey* ‖ *1 tablespoon orange flower water* ‖ *3 tablespoons lemon juice* ‖ *2–3 tablespoons orange juice* ‖ *1 tablespoon ground or grated almonds* ‖ *½ teaspoon salt* ‖ *1 lb carrots, peeled and grated* ‖ *2 oranges, each peeled and cut into 8–10 pieces* ‖ *1 teaspoon extra virgin olive oil* ‖ *2 tablespoons pine nuts* ‖ *mint leaves, to garnish (optional)*

ONE Put the honey in a serving dish, then mix in the flower water and lemon and orange juices. Add the almonds, salt, carrots, and oranges. **TWO** Heat the oil in a small pan and sauté the pine nuts until golden; remove from pan and add to the salad. **THREE** Toss the salad, garnish with mint (if using), and serve; alternatively, chill for later use.

Serves 4–5

NUTRIENT ANALYSIS PER SERVING 196 cal – 818 kJ – 4 g protein – 26 g carbohydrate – 25 g sugars – 9 g fat – 1 g saturates – 5 g fiber – 0.3 g sodium

HEALTHY TIP Rich in fiber, this salad contains a wealth of vitamins as well as the powerful antioxidants betacarotene (pro-vitamin A) and vitamin C, both of which protect the body and help to keep degenerative diseases at bay.

Navy bean salad

I first ate this fresh-tasting salad when visiting the graceful Imperial city of Meknès. It came accompanied by potato and zucchini salads and briouats with chicken (*see page 138*, but these are made with lamb). Once the beans have been soaked, the dish is simple to make. In Morocco, they boil the soaked beans for a few minutes, drain them, cover with fresh water, and cook until soft. This is said to cut down on their gas.

INGREDIENTS *1 cup dried navy beans, soaked 6 hours* ‖ *2 cups water* ‖ *½ medium onion, grated* ‖ *piece fresh root ginger* ‖ *1 medium tomato, peeled, seeded, and sliced into chunks* ‖ *½ tablespoon extra virgin olive oil* ‖ *½ teaspoon turmeric* ‖ *2 teaspoons organic apple cider vinegar* ‖ *½ teaspoon salt* ‖ *pinch black pepper* ‖ *flat leaf parsley sprigs, to garnish (optional)*

ONE Drain the beans and rinse well, then put in a pan with the water. Bring slowly to a boil, skimming the surface as foam forms; reduce heat to very low, cover, and simmer for 20 minutes. **TWO** Add the onions, ginger, tomatoes, and oil and simmer, covered, for 15 minutes or until the beans are tender. **THREE** A few minutes before the end of the cooking time, mash the tomatoes against the side of the pan, then add the turmeric, vinegar, salt, and pepper. Remove pan from heat, cover, and let sit until it cools to room temperature, then remove the ginger. Serve, garnished with parsley sprigs, if using.

Serves 2–4

NUTRIENT ANALYSIS PER SERVING 338 cal – 1436 kJ – 23 g protein – 57 g carbohydrate – 9 g sugars – 4 g fat – 1 g saturates – 25 g fiber – 0.8 g sodium

HEALTHY TIP Navy beans are rich in calcium, magnesium, chromium, copper, iron, and fiber as well as the B vitamins.

Tomato, cucumber, and bell pepper salad

This is a nutritious salad that can be consumed throughout the year. It is good with Kefta (*see page 80*) or as an accompaniment to other salads.

INGREDIENTS *1 garlic clove* ‖ *1 teaspoon salt, or to taste* ‖ *4 mint leaves* ‖ *2 tablespoons lemon juice* ‖ *2 tablespoons extra virgin olive oil* ‖ *1 small onion, sliced into rings* ‖ *1 lb tomatoes, peeled, seeded, and diced* ‖ *1 medium green bell pepper, cored, seeded, and diced* ‖ *½ small cucumber, unpeeled and diced* ‖ *handful finely chopped parsley* ‖ *pinch black pepper (optional)*

ONE To make the dressing, put the garlic, salt, and mint in a mortar and pound with a pestle until creamy. Gradually incorporate the lemon juice and oil. **TWO** Put the onions, tomatoes, bell pepper, cucumber, and parsley in a salad bowl and sprinkle with pepper, if using. **THREE** Add the dressing and toss well before serving.

Serves 4

NUTRIENT ANALYSIS PER SERVING 88 cal – 365 kJ – 3 g protein – 6 g carbohydrate – 5 g sugars – 6 g fat – 1 g saturates – 2 g fiber – 0.5 g sodium (if using 1 teaspoon salt)

HEALTHY TIP The potent nutrients in this salad aid in preventing cancer and other degenerative diseases. It is rich in fiber, C and E vitamins, antioxidants (betacarotene and lycopene), and the minerals sulfur and phosphorus.

Fava bean and cilantro salad

In Morocco, fava beans figure in many dishes such as (when in season) Couscous with Seven Vegetables (*see page 132*) and artichoke salads. In their dried form they are included in the nutritious Berber dish *Urkimen* (*see page 120*). They are also mentioned in the 13th-century cook book of Ibn Razine al-Tujibi. This salad is simple, quick to make, and very tasty. Fresh fava beans, when in season, are excellent—if you have the patience to shell them; otherwise, buy good-quality frozen fava beans. Serve with Orange, Black Olive, and Watercress Salad (*see page 51*).

INGREDIENTS *1 lb fresh shelled or frozen fava beans* ‖ *3 garlic cloves, unpeeled* ‖ *1¼ tablespoons lemon juice, or to taste* ‖ *1½ tablespoons extra virgin olive oil* ‖ *½–¾ teaspoon salt, or to taste* ‖ *black pepper, to taste* ‖ *dash ground cumin (optional)* ‖ *handful cilantro leaves, finely chopped*

ONE Put the shelled fresh fava beans in a steamer with the garlic and steam for 4–5 minutes. If using frozen beans, rinse them slightly to remove any ice, drain, and steam for 6–8 minutes. **TWO** Remove from heat and, if you have the patience, skin the beans (this will take 10–15 minutes but is highly recommended). Place in a serving bowl. **THREE** Peel the garlic, mash, and mix with the lemon juice and oil. Sprinkle the salt, pepper, cumin (if using), and cilantro over the fava beans, then drizzle with the oil mixture. Toss and serve.

Serves 2–4

NUTRIENT ANALYSIS PER SERVING 230 cal – 957 kJ – 15 g protein – 19 g carbohydrate – 4 g sugars – 11 g fat – 1 g saturates – 2 g fiber – 0.5 g sodium (if using ½ teaspoon salt)

HEALTHY TIP This dish is extremely beneficial to those with diabetes. It's very rich in B vitamins and potassium. However, note that favism (a form of anemia) and other conditions can occur in some people who eat the inner part of the fava bean in its raw state.

Three pepper salad

Placing the bell peppers on a heat diffuser over a gas flame cooks them in minutes, locking in most of their nutrients and flavor. In Morocco, peppers are much appreciated and are prepared in various ways. They are usually fried and are then generally eaten hot, but broiling them is a much healthier way to cook them. Serve as an appetizer or to accompany Chicken in a Marinade of Aromatic Spices (*see page 66*) or Poussin in Aromatic Sauce (*see page 62*).

INGREDIENTS *8 oz green bell peppers* ‖ *8 oz red bell peppers* ‖ *8 oz yellow bell peppers* ‖ *1 small garlic clove* ‖ *½ teaspoon salt, or to taste* ‖ *1 teaspoon organic apple cider vinegar* ‖ *1¼ tablespoons lemon juice* ‖ *1¼–1½ tablespoons extra virgin olive oil* ‖ *¼ teaspoon ground cumin, or to taste* ‖ *handful parsley or cilantro leaves, finely chopped* ‖ *pinch black pepper (optional)*

ONE Place the peppers on a heat diffuser over a medium gas flame. Turn them for 3–5 minutes to char all over. Alternatively, preheat the broiler to high, then broil the peppers for 18 minutes or until charred on all sides. Let cool, then peel, core, and seed. Slice the flesh into julienne strips. **TWO** Meanwhile, cream the garlic and salt in a mortar with a pestle. Incorporate the vinegar, lemon juice, and oil and add to the peppers. Sprinkle with the cumin, parsley or cilantro, and pepper, if using. Toss, taste and adjust the seasonings if necessary, then serve.

Serves 4

NUTRIENT ANALYSIS PER SERVING 100 cal – 420 kJ – 3 g protein – 8 g carbohydrate – 8 g sugars – 6 g fat – 1 g saturates – 3 g fiber – 0.3 g sodium (if using ½ teaspoon salt)

HEALTHY TIP This salad is a gold mine of cancer-fighting nutrients. It is rich in carotenoids, vitamin C, betacarotene, and silicon (which is good for forming collagen and healthy nails, skin, and hair). It is also anti-aging.

Olive salad

Here is a tasty salad with warm flavors that doesn't take long to prepare. Writing about olives reminds me of a story. At a party, one of the guests was very busy eating all the olives. A fellow guest got annoyed about his greedy behavior, so he approached him and said: "I would like to attract your attention to the fact that eating too many olives is bad for you. They will make you lose your memory." The guest replied: "You know, you're quite right, because each time I take an olive, I have already forgotten the one I ate before."

INGREDIENTS *7 oz mixed olives, pitted and rinsed* ‖ *1 tablespoon lemon juice* ‖ *2 tablespoons orange juice* ‖ *1 teaspoon extra virgin olive oil* ‖ *½ teaspoon ground cumin* ‖ *¼ teaspoon paprika* ‖ *good pinch ground ginger* ‖ *thin shreds red bell pepper*

ONE Mix the olives with the lemon and orange juices, oil, cumin, paprika, and ginger. Toss with the red bell pepper and serve with bread.

Serves 4

NUTRIENT ANALYSIS PER SERVING 63 cal – 259 kJ – 1 g protein – 1 g carbohydrate – 1 g sugars – 6 g fat – 1 g saturates – 2 g fiber – 1.1 g sodium

HEALTHY TIP Olives are an excellent food, rich in monounsaturated fats that aid in reducing bad (LDL) cholesterol. Nevertheless, they should be consumed in moderation, since they are pickled in a lot of salt. Remember to rinse them before use.

Orange, black olive, and watercress salad

Here is a very refreshing and nutritious salad, excellent for eating during cold weather.

INGREDIENTS *3 oranges* ‖ *pinch salt, or to taste* ‖ *3 oz black olives, halved, pitted, and rinsed* ‖ *juice of ½–1 orange, to taste* ‖ *½–¾ tablespoon extra virgin olive oil* ‖ *1 bunch watercress, leaves and tender stems only*

ONE Peel and slice each orange, then cut into small to medium pieces. Place in a serving bowl and sprinkle with salt. **TWO** Add the olives, orange juice, and oil and toss. Add the watercress, toss again, and serve.

Serves 4

NUTRIENT ANALYSIS PER SERVING 87 cal – 365 kJ – 2 g protein – 11 g carbohydrate – 11 g sugars – 4 g fat – 1 g saturates – 3 g fiber – 0.4 g sodium

HEALTHY TIP This salad is rich in pro-vitamin A, vitamins C, B1, B2, and B9, potassium, phosphorus, manganese, magnesium, iron, and pectin, which helps lower bad (LDL) cholesterol and combat fatigue, aids digestion, and protects from certain cancers. The addition of watercress gives a tasty, peppery note and guards the body against pollution and the effects of smoking.

Beet and mango salad

This colorful salad is very refreshing, nutritious, and quick to prepare. It makes an attractive dish for a buffet.

INGREDIENTS *3–4 small to medium raw beets, washed and coarsely grated* ‖ *1–2 mangoes (if possible, Indian), cubed* ‖ *¾ teaspoon confectioners' sugar* ‖ *1 small garlic clove* ‖ *10–12 mint leaves* ‖ *½ teaspoon salt* ‖ *2 tablespoons lime juice* ‖ *2 tablespoons thick plain yogurt with active cultures* ‖ *juice of 2 oranges* ‖ *1 tablespoon extra virgin olive oil* ‖ *heaping ¼ tablespoon orange flower water*

ONE Place the grated beets in a mixing bowl and the mangoes in a smaller bowl. Using a small strainer with fine holes, sprinkle the confectioners' sugar over the beets and mangoes. **TWO** Pound the garlic, mint, and salt in a mortar with a pestle until smooth, then gradually add the lime juice, yogurt, orange juice, oil, and flower water. **THREE** Pour a little more than half the sauce over the beets and toss. Pour the remaining sauce over the mangoes. **FOUR** Place the beets in a serving dish and spread the mangoes and sauce over. Chill for 30 minutes, then serve.

Serves 4

NUTRIENT ANALYSIS PER SERVING 107 cal – 449 kJ – 3 g protein – 14 g carbohydrate – 13 g sugars – 5 g fat – 2 g saturates – 3 g fiber – 0.3 g sodium

HEALTHY TIP This salad is rich in vitamin C, copper, selenium, sulfur and iron. Its potent antioxidants, vitamin C and betacarotene aid in strengthening the body's defenses against stomach, breast, and other cancers. Beets and their leaves and mangoes contain a lot of betacarotene, which beautifies the skin and delays aging. Other valuable nutrients are folic acid, which feeds the brain, and iron, which is needed for the production of hemoglobin, for energy, and oxygenation of the blood.

Couscous and fava bean salad

This dish is a healthy combination of ingredients, complementing one another in vitamins and amino acids. It is also very simple to prepare.

INGREDIENTS *1 lb fresh shelled or frozen fava beans* ‖ *2 garlic cloves, unpeeled* ‖ *½ cup water* ‖ *½ medium onion, grated* ‖ *2 pinches saffron threads, divided* ‖ *pinch paprika* ‖ *1 teaspoon salt, or to taste, divided* ‖ *2 tablespoons finely chopped cilantro leaves* ‖ *1½ tablespoons extra virgin olive oil, divided* ‖ *pinch black pepper* ‖ *2 tablespoons lemon juice* ‖ *1½ cups organic couscous* ‖ *bouquet garni: 2 bay leaves, 1 parsley sprig, 1 cilantro sprig, tied together with kitchen twine* ‖ *pinch turmeric*

ONE If using frozen fava beans, rinse them slightly to remove any ice, then drain. Put the beans, garlic, water, onion, 1 pinch of the saffron, the paprika, and ½ teaspoon of the salt in a medium pan and simmer over low heat for 5–8 minutes. A minute or two before the end of cooking time add the cilantro and ½ tablespoon of the oil, then season with the pepper. Taste a bean to check if it is soft; if not, simmer a few more minutes. Remove from heat. Peel the garlic, mash until creamy, and mix with the bean mixture. Add the lemon juice and let cool. **TWO** Meanwhile, cover the couscous with water. Rake it with your fingers, then drain and immediately spread it evenly over a large tray or shallow pan. Rake the grains with your fingers a few times to aerate them, then let stand for 20–30 minutes until the water is absorbed and the couscous is relatively dry. **THREE** Sprinkle the couscous with the remaining salt and rub the grains gently between your palms, allowing them to fall back into the tray or pan, to break down any lumps. **FOUR** Put about 1¼ cups water, the bouquet garni, the remaining saffron, and the turmeric in the lower part of a couscoussière or pan and bring to a boil. Put the couscous in the perforated top part of the couscoussière, or in a fine strainer, place over the boiling water, and steam for about 30 minutes. **FIVE** When the couscous is cooked, place it in a large dish, remove the bouquet garni, and drizzle with the remaining oil; using a fork or wooden spoon, mix gently to separate the grains. Add the cooled bean mixture and mix thoroughly. Taste and adjust the seasonings, let stand for a few minutes to allow the flavors to come together, then serve.

Serves 4

NUTRIENT ANALYSIS PER SERVING 300 cal – 1255 kJ – 12 g protein – 49 g carbohydrate – 3 g sugars – 8 g fat – 1 g saturates – 5 g fiber – 0.5 g sodium (if using 1 teaspoon salt)

HEALTHY TIP This salad is rich in nutrients that reinforce immunity and vitality and act as a preventive medicine. It is a good source of protein, vitamin E, magnesium, iron, selenium, and fiber.

Chicken

Chicken, couscous, and caramelized onions

Chicken (or lamb or veal) is simmered with aromatic spices, creating a rich stock. The onions are caramelized with butter and honey.

INGREDIENTS *3 cups water ‖ 1 small chicken, cut into 6–8 pieces ‖ bouquet garni: 1 cinnamon stick, 1 bay leaf, 1 cardamom pod, tied together in cheesecloth ‖ 1 medium onion, finely chopped ‖ 3 garlic cloves, crushed ‖ good pinch saffron threads ‖ 1½ teaspoons salt, or to taste, divided ‖ ½ teaspoon ground ginger ‖ ¼ teaspoon black pepper ‖ 1¼ cups couscous ‖ 2 tablespoons extra virgin olive oil, divided ‖ 1 lb onions, sliced ‖ ½ cup raisins ‖ ½ teaspoon ground cinnamon ‖ small pinch freshly grated nutmeg ‖ 1–2 tablespoons honey ‖ scant ½ tablespoon orange flower water or rosewater (optional)*

ONE Put the water and chicken into a medium pan and bring slowly to a boil. Add the bouquet garni, onion, garlic, saffron, and 1¼ teaspoons of the salt. Reduce heat, cover, and simmer for 50–60 minutes or until chicken is tender. Add the ginger and pepper 5 minutes before the end of cooking time. **TWO** Meanwhile, cover the couscous with water. Rake it through with your fingers, then drain and immediately spread it evenly over a large tray or shallow pan. Rake the grains with your fingers a few times to aerate them, then leave for 20–30 minutes until the water is absorbed and the couscous is relatively dry. **THREE** Rub the couscous gently between your palms, allowing it to fall back into the tray or pan, to break up any lumps. Sprinkle with the remaining salt, drizzle with 1 tablespoon of the oil, and rake through the grains. **FOUR** Ladle out 1¼ cups of stock from the pan, pour into a small pan and bring to a rapid boil; turn off the heat and add the couscous. Cover and leave for 10 minutes or until the stock has been absorbed. **FIVE** Heat the remaining oil in a pan and sauté the onions over low heat until lightly golden. Ladle out 1 cup of stock into a small bowl. Pour a little stock into the onions and cook until reduced. Repeat until all the stock has been added and reduced. As the onions soften, increase the heat. **SIX** Add the raisins, cinnamon, and nutmeg, then add the honey and let caramelize for 5–10 minutes. Stir in the flower water or rosewater, if using, and turn off heat. **SEVEN** To serve, place the couscous in a serving dish and top with the onions. Serve the chicken and stock separately.

Serves 4–6

NUTRIENT ANALYSIS PER SERVING 780 cal – 3256 kJ – 46 g protein – 66 g carbohydrate – 32 g sugars – 39 g fat – 9 g saturates – 3 g fiber – 0.7 g sodium (if using 1 teaspoon of salt)

HEALTHY TIP Valuable in A and B vitamins, iron, phosphates, and sulfur, this dish calms the nerves and soothes the spirit.

Chicken with tomatoes in honey

As well as being succulent, Moroccan dishes are easy to make. This dish just needs stirring from time to time. It makes a good family meal, or a main course for a dinner party. It can be prepared ahead of time to step four, then the cinnamon and honey can be added to simmer gently for 10–15 minutes just before serving.

INGREDIENTS *1 tablespoon extra virgin olive oil* ‖ *handful blanched almonds* ‖ *4 boneless, skinless chicken pieces, about 10 oz* ‖ *1 large onion, grated or finely chopped* ‖ *5 large tomatoes, peeled, seeded, and coarsely chopped* ‖ *½ teaspoon saffron threads* ‖ *good pinch black pepper* ‖ *½–¾ teaspoon salt* ‖ *½–¾ teaspoon ground cinnamon* ‖ *1 tablespoon honey*

ONE Heat a pan, add the oil and almonds and sauté until golden. Alternatively, put the almonds on a baking sheet and toast in a preheated oven, 350°F, for about 10 minutes. Remove and set aside. **TWO** Add the chicken to the pan, cover, and sauté over medium-high heat for about 5 minutes, stirring occasionally. When the chicken is golden, reduce heat to medium and let cook, still covered, in its own juices for another 15 minutes, stirring from time to time. **THREE** Stir in the onions and cook for a few more minutes, then add the tomatoes, saffron, pepper, and salt. Cover and simmer for 40 minutes, stirring once or twice. **FOUR** Transfer the chicken to a separate dish and continue simmering the tomatoes until the liquid has almost evaporated. Season with cinnamon and drizzle all over with the honey. **FIVE** Return the chicken to the pan, simmer for a few minutes to warm through, then garnish with the almonds and serve with couscous.

Serves 4

NUTRIENT ANALYSIS PER SERVING 215 kcal – 905 kJ – 19 g protein – 18 g carbohydrate – 16 g sugars – 8 g fat – 2 g saturates – 4 g fiber – 0.3 g sodium

HEALTHY TIP Chicken with tomatoes and honey is a nourishing dish that warms and strengthens the body. It is low in fat and rich in protein, antioxidants, potassium, and easily assimilated sugars.

Chicken, chickpeas, and onions

This dish has a subtle, clean aftertaste and a lovely deep yellow color from the saffron. Saffron plays an important role in Moroccan cuisine—it imparts a unique flavor and gives the dish a bright yellow or orange color, depending on what ingredients it is combined with. As a general rule, using a whole chicken gives the dish more depth of flavor, derived from the bones, neck, and wings. However, breasts or a mixture of breasts and thighs can be used.

INGREDIENTS *1 small chicken, skinned and cut into 4–6 pieces* ‖ *2 cups water* ‖ *1 small celery stick* ‖ *⅓ cup dried chickpeas, soaked overnight* ‖ *1 lb onions, sliced* ‖ *1 teaspoon salt, or to taste* ‖ *¼ teaspoon black pepper* ‖ *½ teaspoon saffron threads* ‖ *½ teaspoon turmeric* ‖ *1 tablespoon extra virgin olive oil* ‖ *large handful chopped parsley*

ONE Put the chicken and water in a pan and bring slowly to a boil, skimming the surface as foam forms. Add the celery, reduce heat to medium, cover, and simmer for 15 minutes. **TWO** Drain, rinse, and skin the chickpeas, then add to the chicken with the onions, salt, pepper, and saffron. Simmer, covered, over medium-low heat for another 40 minutes or until chicken is tender. **THREE** About 5 minutes before the end of cooking time, stir the turmeric into the oil until dispersed, then add to the pan with the parsley. Check the stock—it should have reduced to a little less than half its amount. Serve hot with a mixed salad and a baked potato.

Serves 4–6

NUTRIENT ANALYSIS PER SERVING 343 cal – 3256 kJ – 42 g protein – 19 g carbohydrate – 8 g sugars – 12 g fat – 3 g saturates – 5 g fiber – 0.7 g sodium (if using 1 teaspoon salt)

HEALTHY TIP Chicken meat shouldn't be underestimated—it is very nourishing and an excellent source of digestible protein. It contains a valuable amount of A, B1, B2, and B3 vitamins and has a good amount of phosphates, magnesium, iron, and zinc. Removing the skin lowers its fat content, and combining it with chickpeas increases its B vitamins.

Poussin in aromatic sauce

Here is one of the easiest Moroccan recipes to make, but you need to prepare it the night before. This way of cooking poussin (spring chicken) is delicious, but the recipe can also be prepared with regular chicken pieces or diced chicken. Serve with Tomato, Cucumber, and Bell Pepper Salad (*see page 40*) and green olives.

INGREDIENTS *2 large garlic cloves* ‖ *1 teaspoon salt* ‖ *2 tablespoons cilantro leaves* ‖ *½ teaspoon ground coriander* ‖ *¼ teaspoon ground cumin* ‖ *¼–½ teaspoon caraway seeds* ‖ *good pinch black pepper* ‖ *2 tablespoons extra virgin olive oil* ‖ *2 tablespoons lemon juice* ‖ *1 tablespoon water* ‖ *½ teaspoon honey* ‖ *2 poussins* ‖ *1 lb potatoes, cut into thick chunks*

ONE To make the marinade, put the garlic, salt, and cilantro leaves in a mortar and pound with a pestle until smooth. **TWO** Add the ground coriander, cumin, caraway, and pepper and mix to a creamy consistency, then gradually add the oil, lemon juice, water, and honey; stir to mix. **THREE** Slice each poussin along its backbone, open, and, using the heel of your hand, flatten the bird. Rub the poussins all over with some of the marinade, then rub the potatoes with the remaining marinade. Cover and refrigerate overnight. **FOUR** Put the poussins and potatoes in a baking dish and bake in a preheated oven, 350°F, for 1 hour or until the poussins and potatoes are cooked through and browned all over.

Serves 2–4

NUTRIENT ANALYSIS PER SERVING 828 cal – 3460 kJ – 56 g protein – 46 g carbohydrate – 4 g sugars – 48 g fat – 11 g saturates – 4 g fiber – 1.2 g sodium

HEALTHY TIP Chicken is rich in protein, which immunizes the body against disease.

Chicken treed

This tasty, healthy dish is said to date from the 7th century and is believed to have been a favorite of the prophet Mohammed. Instead of the pastry, try using one marquq (flatbread) loaf, cut into 8 pieces.

INGREDIENTS *1 tablespoon extra virgin olive oil ‖ 1 medium chicken, skinned and cut into 4–6 pieces, or 4–6 skinless chicken pieces ‖ 5 cups water ‖ 1 lb onions, sliced ‖ 3 garlic cloves, crushed ‖ good pinch saffron threads ‖ 1 cinnamon stick ‖ 1 bay leaf ‖ ¾ teaspoon ground ginger, divided ‖ 1¼ teaspoons salt, or to taste ‖ ½ cup brown lentils ‖ 3 tablespoons split dried fava beans, soaked 10 minutes and drained ‖ pinch black pepper ‖ ½ teaspoon turmeric ‖ ½ teaspoon ground cinnamon (optional) ‖ 1 teaspoon confectioners' sugar (optional)*

DOUGH *2 cups all-purpose flour ‖ ½ teaspoon salt ‖ about ⅔ cup warm water, or as needed ‖ 3 tablespoons olive oil, plus extra for greasing*

ONE Heat the oil in a large pan and sauté the chicken for a few minutes, turning to brown on all sides. Add the water and bring slowly to a boil, skimming the surface as foam forms. Add the onions, garlic, saffron, cinnamon stick, bay leaf, half the ginger, the salt, lentils, and fava beans. Reduce heat to medium-low, cover, and simmer for 40–50 minutes or until chicken is tender. Toward the end of cooking time add the remaining ginger, the pepper, and turmeric. **TWO** Meanwhile, make the dough. Put the flour and salt in a bowl, gradually add the water, and knead very thoroughly for about 15 minutes. Pinch off pieces of the dough to form small balls, place in a tray with the oil, and turn to coat with the oil. Keeping your hands oiled, flatten each ball, pressing down with the heel of your hand and pulling the dough out all around to form a round as thin as possible. **THREE** Heat a heavy nonstick pan, then add one pastry sheet—it will dry immediately. Turn it over to dry the other side (do not brown), then remove from pan and repeat with remaining sheets. **FOUR** To serve, place 1 or 2 sheets in each dish and top with some chicken, onions, lentils, and beans. Sprinkle with cinnamon and confectioners' sugar, if using. Fold the sheets over to enclose the filling, then top with some of the stock.

Serves 4

NUTRIENT ANALYSIS PER SERVING 619 cal – 2604 kJ – 46 g protein – 73 g carbohydrate – 9 g sugars – 18 g fat – 4 g saturates – 4 g fiber – 1 g sodium (if using 1¾ teaspoons salt)

HEALTHY TIP This dish is very rich in A, B, and E vitamins, phosphorus, iron, zinc, quercetin, selenium, and germanium. Whenever I eat it, my sleep is never interrupted.

Chicken in a marinade of aromatic spices

This recipe, inspired by a recipe from a 13th-century cook book by Ibn Razine al-Tujibi, is a delicious way to prepare chicken. It is simple and nutritious, and the smell of the spices that wafts around the house really whets the appetite. You need to marinate the chicken overnight. Serve with Grated Carrot and Orange Salad (*see page 34*), or Lettuce and Orange Salad (*see page 32*) and Cucumber and Nut Salad (*see page 38*).

INGREDIENTS *2–3 large garlic cloves* ‖ *½–1 teaspoon freshly grated ginger root* ‖ *1 tablespoon thyme* ‖ *1 teaspoon salt* ‖ *¼ teaspoon black pepper* ‖ *¼–½ teaspoon turmeric* ‖ *¼ tablespoon lemon juice* ‖ *1 teaspoon organic apple cider vinegar* ‖ *1½ tablespoons extra virgin olive oil* ‖ *2 tablespoons water* ‖ *1 lb boneless, skinless chicken breasts, diced*

ONE To make the marinade, cream the garlic, ginger, thyme, and salt in a mortar with a pestle, then add the pepper and turmeric. Gradually add the lemon juice, vinegar, oil, and water and mix thoroughly until you have a smooth texture. Rub the chicken pieces all over with the marinade, cover, and refrigerate overnight. **TWO** Remove the chicken from the refrigerator and let stand at room temperature for a few minutes, then put into a baking dish and bake in a preheated oven, 350°F, for 20 minutes or until browned all over but not dry. Serve with a salad (see above).

Serves 3–5

NUTRIENT ANALYSIS PER SERVING 253 cal – 1063 kJ – 37 g protein – 2 g carbohydrate – 0 g sugars – 11 g fat – 3 g saturates – 0 g fiber – 0.8 g sodium

HEALTHY TIP This dish is low in fat and rich in protein, niacin, riboflavin, thiamine, monounsaturated fats, phosphorus, zinc, and antioxidants.

Tagine of chicken with potatoes, cilantro, and olives

This is a comforting family meal. In Morocco, potatoes are considered winter food; in the cold weather, this dish provides the warmth the body needs at that time of year. This dish is easy to make; serve with bread and a side salad.

INGREDIENTS *1 small to medium chicken, cut into 4–6 pieces, or 4 chicken breasts or mixed portions* ‖ *2 cups water* ‖ *1–2 bay leaves* ‖ *1 medium onion, grated* ‖ *1 teaspoon salt, or to taste* ‖ *pinch saffron threads* ‖ *3 garlic cloves, crushed* ‖ *½ teaspoon ground ginger* ‖ *1 tablespoon extra virgin olive oil, divided* ‖ *2 lb potatoes, scrubbed and cubed* ‖ *large handful finely chopped cilantro leaves* ‖ *2 thyme sprigs* ‖ *about 10 black or green olives, pitted and rinsed (optional)* ‖ *pinch black pepper* ‖ *2 tablespoons lemon juice, or to taste*

ONE Place the chicken and water in a medium pan and bring slowly to a boil, skimming the surface as foam forms. Add the bay leaves, onions, salt, saffron, garlic, ginger, and 1 teaspoon of the oil. Reduce heat to medium-low; simmer for 25–30 minutes. **TWO** Add the potatoes and continue cooking until potatoes and chicken are tender, checking the water level and adding a little more hot water if necessary. About 5 minutes before the end of cooking time, add the cilantro, thyme, olives (if using), pepper, and the remaining oil. **THREE** Drizzle with the lemon juice and serve with crusty bread and a salad.

Serves 4

NUTRIENT ANALYSIS PER SERVING 440 cal – 1863 kJ – 40 g protein – 52 g carbohydrate – 5 g sugars – 10 g fat – 2 g saturates – 6 g fiber – 1 g sodium (if using 1 teaspoon salt)

HEALTHY TIP This tagine is a good source of protein, potassium, selenium, iron, B vitamins, and phosphorus.

Chicken, chickpeas, and raisins

This is a comforting and energizing dish. It has subtle flavors in spite of the powerful aroma of saffron. The turmeric bestows a beautiful pale color to the liquor.

INGREDIENTS *⅓ cup dried chickpeas, soaked overnight, or 13 oz canned chickpeas, drained and rinsed* ‖ *3 cups water* ‖ *2½ small to medium onions* ‖ *1 medium chicken, skinned and cut into 4–6 pieces* ‖ *bouquet garni: 1 celery stick, 1 bay leaf, 1 large cinnamon stick, tied together with kitchen twine* ‖ *a few saffron threads* ‖ *¼–½ cup raisins* ‖ *¼ teaspoon turmeric* ‖ *1½ cups organic couscous* ‖ *salt and black pepper*

ONE If using dried chickpeas drain and rinse well. Put in a medium pan with the water and bring slowly to a boil, skimming the surface as foam forms. Reduce heat to low, cover, and simmer for 2½ hours or until nearly soft. **TWO** Meanwhile, coarsely slice 1½ onions and grate the remaining onion. If using canned chickpeas, bring the water to a boil and add chickpeas, grated onion, chicken, bouquet garni, and saffron. Bring to a boil, reduce heat to low, cover, and simmer for 10 minutes. **THREE** Add the sliced onions and raisins to the pan. Bring to a boil, reduce the heat, cover, and simmer for another 20 minutes. Spoon a little of the stock into a bowl and stir in the turmeric until dissolved. Add to the pan and cook for 10 more minutes or until chicken is tender. Remove bouquet garni. **FOUR** Meanwhile, cover the couscous with water. Rake it with your fingers, drain, and immediately spread it evenly over a large tray or shallow pan. Rake the grains with your fingers a few times to aerate them, then leave for 20–30 minutes until the water is absorbed and the couscous is relatively dry. **FIVE** Rub the couscous gently between your palms, allowing it to fall back into the tray or pan, to break down any lumps. **SIX** Measure 2 cups of the stock into a pan, taste and adjust seasonings, and bring to a rapid boil. Remove from heat and quickly add couscous; cover and let stand for 10 minutes or until stock has been fully absorbed. **SEVEN** To serve, place the couscous in a circle on a serving plate and pile the chicken in the middle. Serve the remaining sauce alongside. Serve hot or warm.

Serves 4–6

NUTRIENT ANALYSIS PER SERVING 498 cal – 2099 kJ – 49 g protein – 67 g carbohydrate – 18 g sugars – 6 g fat – 1 g saturates – 5 g fiber – 0.2 g sodium

HEALTHY TIP This dish is high in protein and B vitamins, including inositol and choline (important for the nervous system, hair growth, and for reducing bad (LDL) cholesterol). It is also rich in phosphorus, iron, potassium, magnesium, zinc, copper, quercetin, and calcium.

Tagine of chicken and olives

Here is an ideal combination of chicken and olives. It is flavorful and rich in good fats that satisfy the palate and calm the appetite. Like most other dishes in this book, it is of utmost simplicity. Serve with bread and roasted potatoes.

INGREDIENTS *1 small to medium chicken, cut into 3–4 pieces* ‖ *1¼ cups water* ‖ *1 slice lemon* ‖ *good pinch saffron threads* ‖ *4 garlic cloves, crushed* ‖ *pinch salt* ‖ *1 teaspoon extra virgin olive oil* ‖ *½ teaspoon ground ginger, divided* ‖ *½ teaspoon paprika* ‖ *¼ teaspoon ground cumin* ‖ *7 oz pitted green olives, rinsed* ‖ *2 tablespoons lemon juice*

ONE Put the chicken and water in a medium pan and bring slowly to a boil, skimming the surface as foam forms. Add the lemon, saffron, garlic, salt, oil, and half the ginger. Reduce heat to medium, cover, and simmer for 50–60 minutes or until chicken is tender. **TWO** Add the remaining ginger, the paprika, and cumin and stir gently—try not to break up the chicken. Alternatively, remove the chicken and bone, then return it to the sauce—you should have about ⅔ cup or a little more. Add the olives and lemon juice, simmer for about 5 minutes, then serve hot.

Serves 4–5

NUTRIENT ANALYSIS PER SERVING 488 cal – 2025 kJ – 41 g protein – 1 g carbohydrate – 0 g sugars – 36 g fat – 9 g saturates – 2 g fiber – 1.2 g sodium

HEALTHY TIP This dish is rich in the antiwrinkle vitamin A, the B vitamins, selenium, phosphorus, sulfur, and zinc. Olives are excellent for the heart, as they are naturally low in sodium. Nevertheless, they must be consumed in moderation, since they're pickled in salt.

B'steeya with chicken
While I was in Fez, Madame Sefraoui kindly explained the stages of this recipe.

INGREDIENTS *1 small to medium chicken, cut into 4 pieces* ‖ *2 cups water* ‖ *2 large cinnamon sticks* ‖ *1½ lb onions, finely chopped* ‖ *1½ teaspoons salt, or to taste* ‖ *good pinch saffron threads* ‖ *2 large handfuls finely chopped parsley* ‖ *1 large handful finely chopped cilantro leaves* ‖ *¼–1 teaspoon ground ginger* ‖ *¼ teaspoon black pepper* ‖ *½ teaspoon turmeric* ‖ *1½ tablespoons extra virgin olive oil, divided, plus extra for greasing* ‖ *4 eggs (1 separated)* ‖ *1¼ cups blanched almonds* ‖ *1¼ tablespoons confectioners' sugar, or to taste, divided* ‖ *1 heaping teaspoon ground cinnamon, divided* ‖ *7 sheets filo pastry*

ONE Put the chicken and water in a pan and bring slowly to a boil, skimming the surface as foam forms. Add the cinnamon sticks, onions, and salt, cover, and simmer until the onions have reduced in size. Add the saffron and cook for 30 minutes. **TWO** Add the parsley, cilantro, ginger, pepper, turmeric, and 1 tablespoon of the oil; cover and simmer for 15–20 more minutes or until chicken is tender. **THREE** Remove the chicken and let cool slightly. Discard the skin and bones and cut the meat into bite-sized pieces. **FOUR** Transfer just less than half the onion mixture to a small dish. Beat 3 eggs and 1 egg white, add to the sauce in the pan, and cook, stirring continuously, for 5 minutes or until set to a thick consistency. Let cool. **FIVE** Brown the almonds on a baking sheet in a preheated oven, 350°F, for 10–15 minutes. Remove from oven and sprinkle with 1 teaspoon of the confectioners' sugar and ¼ teaspoon of the cinnamon. Let cool, then chop coarsely. **SIX** Place one filo sheet horizontally across a greased 12 inch pan and another across vertically. Fold another sheet in half and place over the other sheets. Spread with the almonds. Fold another sheet in half and place over the almonds, then spread the egg sauce over that. Mix the chicken with the remaining sauce and spread over the eggs. Sprinkle with the remaining cinnamon and 2 teaspoons of the confectioners' sugar. Fold in the overhanging edges, cover with 2–3 more filo sheets and gently tuck underneath to form a neat round shape. Brush with the remaining oil and egg yolk, beaten. Bake on the lower shelf of a preheated oven, 375°F, for 30–40 minutes or until golden. **SEVEN** Sprinkle with the remaining confectioners' sugar and serve.

Serves 6–8

NUTRIENT ANALYSIS PER SERVING 824 cal – 3424 kJ – 48 g protein – 37 g carbohydrate – 12 g sugars – 55 g fat – 10 g saturates – 8 g fiber – 0.8 g sodium (if using 1½ teaspoons salt)

HEALTHY TIP *B'steeya* is a rich source of protein, E and B vitamins, magnesium, potassium, phosphorus, quercetin, and sulfur. This powerful mixture builds resistance against cancer, aids circulation, and detoxifies the organs.

Steamed chicken stuffed with aromatic rice

This dish requires a bit of time to prepare, but it is not at all difficult, and frankly I never bother to truss the chicken. In Morocco, a variety of stuffings are used—couscous with almonds and raisins, for instance. I love to stuff it with coarse bulgar or, like in this recipe, with rice.

INGREDIENTS *1 small to medium chicken ‖ finely chopped pitted black olives and finely chopped red bell peppers, to garnish ‖ salt and black pepper (optional)*

STUFFING *1 cup brown basmati rice, rinsed once and drained ‖ 2 tomatoes, peeled, seeded, and chopped ‖ 2 tablespoons finely chopped parsley ‖ 2 tablespoons finely chopped cilantro leaves ‖ 1 heaping teaspoon finely chopped thyme ‖ ½ teaspoon turmeric ‖ ½ teaspoon ground cumin ‖ 1 teaspoon salt ‖ 1 tablespoon extra virgin olive oil ‖ 1 tablespoon lemon juice*

ONE If you desire, rub the chicken with a little salt and pepper. Thoroughly mix all the ingredients for the stuffing together and stuff the chicken at the neck end. Pull the neck flap over the stuffing to cover and, if you desire, secure with a toothpick. **TWO** Fill the bottom half of a couscoussière or pan a little more than half full with water and bring to a boil. Put the chicken in the perforated top section of the couscoussière or in a steamer and place over the boiling water. Cover and steam for 1½ hours. **THREE** Check the rice in the stuffing. If it's cooked, remove the pan; otherwise, leave for a little longer. **FOUR** Transfer the chicken to a hot dish. Mix the olives with the red peppers, garnish the chicken, and serve.

Serves 4–6

NUTRIENT ANALYSIS PER SERVING 375 cal – 1570 kJ – 19 g protein – 38 g carbohydrate – 3 g sugars – 17 g fat – 4g saturates – 3 g fiber – 0.9 g sodium

HEALTHY TIP This nutritious, one-pot meal is wholesome and strengthens and beautifies skin and hair. It is an excellent source of protein, which is indispensable for growth and immunity, intellect, and much more; B vitamins which are important for the nervous system; iron, a deficiency of which creates fatigue and reduces mental capacity; zinc, which keeps the immune system in great shape; and potassium, to regulate blood pressure. The mixture of herbs and spices adds flavor but also has antioxidant properties, especially the turmeric, while thyme is known to activate the brain and is an antiseptic.

Lamb tagine with dried plums and apricots

This dish brings to mind the cultural, religious, medieval city of Fez, which I visited during their festival of culinary arts. While there, I tasted many delicious tagines, among them a specialty from the north with veal, apricots, and walnuts, and another from the south with figs and walnuts. Despite its sweetness, I like to eat this with baked sweet potato and plain couscous or bulgar.

INGREDIENTS *½ tablespoon olive oil ‖ handful blanched almonds ‖ 4 lamb shanks or 1 lb boneless lamb from the knuckle ‖ 1 medium onion, chopped ‖ 1¼ teaspoons ground ginger ‖ 30 coriander seeds, ground ‖ ¼ teaspoon ground saffron ‖ ¼ teaspoon black pepper ‖ 1 teaspoon turmeric ‖ ½ teaspoon salt ‖ 1 large cinnamon stick ‖ ¾–1¼ cups hot water ‖ 12 dried plums, soaked and drained ‖ 2 slices orange rind ‖ heaping ¾ teaspoon ground cinnamon ‖ 1 tablespoon honey ‖ 1 teaspoon clarified butter (see page 14) ‖ 4 dried apricots, soaked and drained ‖ pinch freshly grated nutmeg ‖ 1 tablespoon orange flower water ‖ large handful cilantro leaves ‖ 1 tablespoon toasted sesame seeds, to garnish*

ONE Heat a pan over medium heat, add the oil and almonds; sauté until golden. Add the lamb and onions and sauté until brown. Add the ginger, ground coriander, saffron, pepper, turmeric, salt, and cinnamon stick, stir for a few seconds, then add the hot water and bring to a boil (the amount of water depends on the quality of the meat—the better the meat, the less water it will need). Reduce heat to low, cover, and simmer for 1 hour or until the meat is very tender. **TWO** Add the dried plums, orange rind, and ground cinnamon and bring to a boil; reduce the heat, cover, and simmer for 15–20 minutes. **THREE** Add the honey, butter, apricots, nutmeg, flower water, and cilantro, increase the heat and let bubble for about 10 minutes until caramelized, but do not allow the mixture to dry out. **FOUR** Remove from heat and let stand for 5 minutes for the flavors to mellow (the sauce must be concentrated), remove the cinnamon stick, then garnish with the sesame seeds and serve.

Serves 4

NUTRIENT ANALYSIS PER SERVING 383 cal – 1604 kJ – 29 g protein – 22 g carbohydrate – 21 g sugars – 20 g fat – 8 g saturates – 6 g fiber – 0.4 g sodium

HEALTHY TIP Apricots are rich in betacarotene and lycopene (good for the eyes). Adding an apple would also be good, as it would counterbalance the saturated fatty acids of the meat and butter. The pectin in the apricots thickens the liquor, but most important, it slows the absorption of sugars into the bloodstream and gives a sense of fullness.

Kefta with aromatic herbs

This dish makes an excellent meal eaten with Tomato, Cucumber, and Bell Pepper Salad *(see page 40)* or, for a variation, try adding the Keftas to Aromatic Tomato Sauce *(see below)* and simmering for 5 minutes before serving.

INGREDIENTS *½ medium onion* ‖ *2½ oz parsley* ‖ *2½ oz cilantro leaves* ‖ *1 teaspoon ground cumin* ‖ *1 teaspoon paprika* ‖ *heaping ¼ teaspoon cayenne pepper* ‖ *1 teaspoon salt* ‖ *1 lb lean ground lamb*

ONE Put all ingredients except meat in a food processor and pulse briefly. Add the meat and pulse again until mixed. Alternatively, grate the onion, chop the parsley and cilantro finely, and mix with the other ingredients. **TWO** Divide into 18–24 pieces and roll each into a ball. Mold each ball around a skewer, pressing the meat gently yet firmly into a sausage shape. **THREE** Place under a preheated hot broiler and cook for 3–5 minutes on each side until browned.

Serves 4

NUTRIENT ANALYSIS PER SERVING 220 cal – 923 kJ – 27 g protein – 2 g carbohydrate – 2 g sugars – 12 g fat – 5 g saturates – 2 g fiber – 0.6 g sodium

HEALTHY TIP This dish is rich in protein, iron, betacarotene, vitamin C, phosphorus, zinc, and potassium.

Aromatic tomato sauce

INGREDIENTS *2¼ lb tomatoes, peeled, seeded, and chopped* ‖ *1 teaspoon salt* ‖ *½ teaspoon saffron threads* ‖ *1 small onion, grated* ‖ *1½ tablespoons extra virgin olive oil* ‖ *¼ teaspoon black pepper* ‖ *¼–½ teaspoon cayenne pepper* ‖ *handful finely chopped parsley or cilantro leaves*

ONE Stir the tomatoes, salt, saffron, onions, and oil together in a pan and simmer until mixture reaches a medium-thick consistency. **TWO** Sprinkle with the pepper, cayenne, and parsley or cilantro and simmer for another 1–2 minutes.

Serves 6

NUTRIENT ANALYSIS PER SERVING 68 cal – 88 kJ – 2 g protein – 8 g carbohydrate – 7 g sugars – 4 g fat – 1 g saturates – 3 g fiber – 0.4 g sodium

Tagine of lamb and artichokes with rice

Moroccans are fond of artichoke tagine, which has a delicate and tasty flavor. This recipe was given to me during my stay in Rabat, the capital of Morocco. Fresh artichokes do take a little time to prepare, but they are worth it for their flavor.

INGREDIENTS *1 lb boneless lamb (leg or shoulder), cut into medium-sized pieces* ‖ *4½ cups water, divided* ‖ *1 teaspoon salt, or to taste* ‖ *1 bay leaf* ‖ *1 cinnamon stick* ‖ *1 medium onion, sliced* ‖ *3 large garlic cloves, crushed* ‖ *good pinch saffron threads* ‖ *¾ tablespoon, plus 1 teaspoon extra virgin olive oil* ‖ *4 fresh artichokes or 4 canned artichoke hearts* ‖ *lemon juice* ‖ *¼ teaspoon black pepper* ‖ *good pinch freshly grated root ginger* ‖ *1 oz finely chopped parsley* ‖ *½ cup finely chopped cilantro leaves* ‖ *2 cups water* ‖ *¾ teaspoon salt, or to taste* ‖ *½ teaspoon turmeric* ‖ *1 cup basmati rice, rinsed once and drained*

ONE Put the lamb and 2½ cups water in a medium pan and bring slowly to a boil, skimming the surface as foam forms. Add the salt, bay leaf, cinnamon stick, onions, garlic, saffron, and ¾ tablespoon oil and return to a boil. Reduce heat, cover, and simmer for 40 minutes. **TWO** Meanwhile, if using fresh artichokes, remove all the leaves (set aside to steam later). Using a pointed knife, remove and discard the choke from the center of each artichoke. Trim the heart, rinse with cold water, and rub with lemon juice to prevent discoloration. **THREE** At the end of the cooking time for the meat, drain the canned artichokes, if using, slice each fresh or canned artichoke heart into quarters, and add to the pan. Bring to a boil, reduce heat, cover, and cook for another 15–20 minutes or until meat is tender. About 5 minutes before the end of cooking time season with the pepper and fresh ginger; add the parsley and cilantro. **FOUR** Meanwhile, cook the rice. Bring 2 cups of the water and salt to a boil, add the turmeric and rice. Reduce heat to low, cover and simmer for 6–7 minutes or until water has been absorbed. A couple of minutes before the rice is ready, gently stir in 1 teaspoon of the oil with a fork. **FIVE** Serve the tagine with the rice.

Serves 4

NUTRIENT ANALYSIS PER SERVING 468 cal – 1958 kJ – 33 g protein – 50 g carbohydrate – 3 g sugars – 15 g fat – 6 g saturates – 1 g fiber – 1 g sodium (if using ¾ teaspoons salt)

HEALTHY TIP Artichokes are low in calories, diuretic, have therapeutic substances, eliminate toxins, and are ideal for diabetics. This dish is also rich in B and C vitamins, potassium, iron, calcium, phosphorus, and magnesium.

Honeyed lamb tagine

This tagine (*Mrouzia*) is the traditional Moroccan dish cooked for Id el-Kabir (big feast), the festival of the sacrifice of Abraham, during which it is customary to distribute meat to the poor. It has an amazing balance of flavors and makes a great lunch or dinner. It is enjoyable and quite therapeutic to prepare. The neck, shoulder, or leg of lamb are all excellent to use, and for a richer flavor, add a lamb bone.

INGREDIENTS ½ tablespoon Ras el-hanout (see page 14) ‖ ½ teaspoon ground ginger ‖ pinch black pepper ‖ ¼ teaspoon ground saffron ‖ ½ teaspoon ground cinnamon ‖ 1 lb boneless lamb (neck, leg, or shoulder), cut into medium to large chunks ‖ ½ cup raisins ‖ 1–2 tablespoons extra virgin olive oil ‖ 1 medium onion, finely chopped ‖ ½ cup blanched almonds ‖ 1 large cinnamon stick ‖ 1 bay leaf ‖ ½ teaspoon salt ‖ 1¼ cups hot water, or as needed ‖ 1 heaping tablespoon honey ‖ 1 teaspoon turmeric (optional)

ONE Put the Ras el-hanout in a small bowl, add the ginger, pepper, saffron, cinnamon, and about a tablespoon of water and mix thoroughly. Rub three-quarters of this spice mixture into the meat, coating it on all sides. Mix the remainder with the raisins. **TWO** Heat the oil in a pan, add the meat, onions, almonds, cinnamon stick, and bay leaf and sprinkle with the salt. Stir together, then cook for 5–7 minutes, stirring occasionally. **THREE** Add the hot water, cover, and simmer over medium heat for about 1 hour or until the meat is very tender, stirring occasionally and checking the water—if necessary, add more hot water. **FOUR** When the meat is tender and the liquid has reduced, add the raisins, honey, and turmeric (if using), and cook for another 5–8 minutes, stirring from time to time to prevent the ingredients from sticking to the pan. **FIVE** Serve hot with roasted or baked potatoes, or couscous and carrot salads (*see pages 33 and 34*).

Serves 3–4

NUTRIENT ANALYSIS PER SERVING 650 cal – 2720 kJ – 40 g protein – 47 g carbohydrate – 44 g sugars – 35 g fat – 9 g saturates – 7 g fiber – 0.5 g sodium

HEALTHY TIP This savory-sweet mélange of meat, almonds, raisins, honey, and spices contains amino acids, vitamins, minerals, and antioxidants important for growth, cell renewal, and much more. It strengthens the immune system and is good for the brain and heart.

Lamb with dates and honey

What an unusual mixture. The meat simmers gently with potent herbs, to which is added the powerful flavors of saffron and cinnamon and the natural sugars of honey and dates. From this amazing blend emerges an excellent velvety texture and soothing taste. All you need are good-quality ingredients and love while cooking it. With these salty-sweet dishes, I like to serve sweet potatoes, rich in carotene, along with an Orange, Black Olive, and Watercress Salad (*see page 51*).

INGREDIENTS *1 tablespoon extra virgin olive oil* ‖ *handful slivered almonds* ‖ *1 lb boneless lamb (leg or shoulder), cut into 4 pieces* ‖ *¾–1¼ cups water* ‖ *1 small onion, finely chopped* ‖ *½ cup chopped cilantro leaves* ‖ *1 large garlic clove, crushed* ‖ *a few fennel slices, about 4 oz* ‖ *½–¾ teaspoon salt* ‖ *½ teaspoon saffron threads* ‖ *1 teaspoon ground cinnamon* ‖ *pinch to ½ teaspoon sugar* ‖ *1 heaping tablespoon honey* ‖ *8 dates (preferably medjool), pitted*

ONE Heat the oil gently in a medium pan and sauté the almonds, stirring continuously, until golden but not too browned. Alternatively, put the almonds on a baking sheet and toast in a preheated oven, 350°F, for about 10 minutes. Remove and set aside. **TWO** Add the lamb to the pan and brown over medium-high heat for about 5 minutes. Add ¾ cup of the water and bring slowly to a boil, skimming the surface as foam forms. Add the onions, cilantro, garlic, fennel, salt, and saffron. Return to a boil, reduce heat to low, cover, and simmer for about 50 minutes or until meat is tender. **THREE** Check the amount of sauce—there should be enough to serve 2–3 tablespoons with each portion. If not, add the extra water. Sprinkle with the cinnamon, sugar, and honey and stir well. Bring to a boil, reduce heat, and simmer for 5 minutes. **FOUR** Add the dates, simmer for another 8–10 minutes until the sauce reaches a medium-thick consistency, then remove from heat and let stand for 5 minutes before serving.

Serves 4

NUTRIENT ANALYSIS PER SERVING 374 cal – 1566 kJ – 28 g protein – 30 g carbohydrate – 12 g sugars – 16 g fat – 6 g saturates – 1 g fiber – 0.4 g sodium

HEALTHY TIP Besides being enriched with vitamins and minerals, this dish strengthens all parts of the body. It is energy giving, diuretic, and calming, very rich in protein, B vitamins, fiber, potassium, magnesium, zinc (which aids a healthy immune system), calcium, phosphates, and the trace element boron. The dates and herbs aid the digestion of the meat.

Tagine of lamb with pumpkin

Here is another delicious way of preparing lamb, and a perfect meal for the cold winter. The flavor of the meat and spices marries well with the delicacy of the pumpkin. The dish can be prepared ahead of time and reheated as needed.

INGREDIENTS *1 lb boneless lamb (leg or shoulder), cut into medium-sized pieces* ‖ *1 tablespoon extra virgin olive oil, divided* ‖ *1 small onion, studded with 1 clove* ‖ *1½ cups water* ‖ *2 garlic cloves, crushed* ‖ *1 bay leaf* ‖ *1 cinnamon stick* ‖ *pinch saffron threads* ‖ *1½ teaspoons salt, divided, or to taste* ‖ *½ teaspoon ground ginger* ‖ *2 lb peeled pumpkin, seeded and cubed* ‖ *1 teaspoon sugar* ‖ *1 teaspoon honey* ‖ *¾ teaspoon turmeric*

ONE Heat a pan, then add the lamb, 1 teaspoon of the oil, and the onion. Stir for a few seconds, then add the water, and bring slowly to a boil, skimming the surface as foam forms. Reduce heat to low, add the garlic, bay leaf, cinnamon stick, saffron, and 1 teaspoon of the salt and simmer for 1 hour or until meat is very tender. Five minutes before the end of cooking time, dissolve the ginger in a little of the lamb stock and add to the pan. **TWO** Meanwhile, put the pumpkin in a large shallow pan, stir in the remaining salt and heat gently. As the pumpkin softens, break it down with the back of a wooden spoon and stir occasionally until the water evaporates. **THREE** Stir in the remaining oil, sprinkle with the sugar and honey, and cook for 8 minutes or until the pumpkin caramelizes. Dissolve the turmeric in a little of the lamb stock, then stir into the pumpkin, cook for few more seconds, and taste and adjust the seasonings. **FOUR** To serve, place the pumpkin purée on a hot serving dish and top with the meat and sauce.

Serves 4

NUTRIENT ANALYSIS PER SERVING 278 cal – 1163 kJ – 28 g protein – 10 g carbohydrate – 8 g sugars – 14 g fat – 6 g saturates – 2 g fiber – 0.8 g sodium (if using 1½ teaspoons salt)

HEALTHY TIP This dish has a good quality of protein and is very rich in minerals such as iron (necessary to produce energy) and zinc and is rich in fiber. It is also high in potent betacarotene and in potassium. It's good for the skin and may aid insomnia.

Tagine of lamb and green beans

While I was in Fez, my guide Hisham took me to a beautifully ornate restaurant where I ate this tagine, which has more sauce than other tagines. Its flavors traveled back with me to London and I prepared it right away. This dish is succulent and wholesome, and so comforting and satisfying that you will want to have more helpings. Serve fruit such as whole apples, pears, or oranges to finish the meal.

INGREDIENTS *1 lb boneless leg of lamb, cut into 8 pieces* ‖ *1¼ teaspoons salt, or to taste* ‖ *⅔ cup water* ‖ *1 tablespoon extra virgin olive oil* ‖ *¼ small onion, sliced* ‖ *good pinch saffron threads, divided* ‖ *½ teaspoon ground ginger, divided* ‖ *½ teaspoon paprika, divided* ‖ *4 tomatoes, peeled, seeded, and chopped* ‖ *2½ lb green beans* ‖ *1 heaping teaspoon tomato paste* ‖ *¾ teaspoon turmeric* ‖ *1½ tablespoons lemon juice*

ONE Place the lamb in a small to medium pan, sprinkle with the salt and rub in, then let stand for 5 minutes. **TWO** Put the pan over medium heat, and when juices start to appear, add the water, oil, onion, and half each of the saffron, ginger, and paprika. Stir for 1–2 minutes, then stir in the tomatoes and top with the beans. Reduce heat to low, cover, and simmer for 1 hour or until meat is tender. Check the water level from time to time and if necessary add a little hot water. **THREE** About 15 minutes before the end of cooking time add the tomato paste. A few minutes before the end of cooking time add the remaining saffron, ginger, and paprika and the turmeric; cover and simmer to finish cooking. **FOUR** Add the lemon juice, shake the pan, and remove from heat. Let stand for a few minutes to allow the flavors to blend, then serve hot with bread.

Serves 3–4

NUTRIENT ANALYSIS PER SERVING 427 cal – 1782 kJ – 43 g protein – 19 g carbohydrate – 15 g sugars – 21 g fat – 8 g saturates – 13 g fiber – 1 g sodium (if using 1¼ teaspoons salt)

HEALTHY TIP We should avoid eating sauces that are rich in saturated fats, and in this dish no butter is used and the meat is extra lean. It's a great source of potent, anticancerous lycopene and other protective nutrients such as A and B vitamins, potassium, phosphorus, zinc, and magnesium—all important for the functioning of enzymes, which augment the ability of intellect and prevent stress. This dish is good for growing children, very active people, and diabetics.

Shoulder of lamb stuffed with couscous
Although the stuffing needs care and the cooking is long and slow, this is a delicious, special dish for entertaining friends or family.

INGREDIENTS *2½ cups organic couscous* ‖ *½ teaspoon salt* ‖ *5¼ cups water, divided* ‖ *½ tablespoon orange flower water* ‖ *¼ cup slivered almonds* ‖ *2 tablespoons raisins* ‖ *pinch freshly grated nutmeg* ‖ *1½ teaspoons ground cinnamon, divided* ‖ *½ tablespoon extra virgin olive oil* ‖ *5 lb shoulder of lamb, boneless* ‖ *a few saffron threads* ‖ *bouquet garni: 1 large cinnamon stick, 1 onion studded with 2 cloves, 2 bay leaves, 1 celery stick* ‖ *good pinch black pepper* ‖ *1 tablespoon honey* ‖ *1 teaspoon fructose (fruit sugar)*

ONE Rinse ¾ cup of the couscous, rake it through with your fingers, then drain and immediately spread it evenly over a large tray or shallow pan. Rake the grains with your fingers a few times to aerate them, then leave for 20–30 minutes until the water is absorbed and the couscous is relatively dry. **TWO** Sprinkle the salt, ¼ cup of the water, the flower water, and almonds over the couscous, rake with your fingers a few times to aerate the grains, and set aside to absorb the liquid. When dry, rub the grains gently between your palms, allowing them to fall back into the tray or pan, to break down any lumps. Add the raisins, nutmeg, ½ teaspoon of the ground cinnamon, and the oil. **THREE** Stuff the bone cavity of the lamb with the couscous mixture and sew or secure to enclose the filling. Put the lamb in a large pan, add 5 cups of the water, and bring slowly to a boil, skimming the surface as foam forms. Add the saffron and bouquet garni, reduce heat to low, and simmer for 2 hours. Turn the meat over and simmer for another 1–2 hours or until very tender. To reduce the saturated fat content, remove from heat and cool, then chill the lamb and stock separately. The next day, remove the solidified fat, reheat the lamb in the stock, and continue as below. **FOUR** Remove the onion, discard the cloves, and press the onion through a strainer over the pan. Discard the remaining bouquet garni ingredients. Sprinkle with the pepper, the remaining ground cinnamon, the honey, and fructose, increase heat, and cook for another 15 minutes until caramelized, but do not let dry out. **FIVE** Ladle 2 cups of the stock into a small pan, bring to a boil, and add the remaining couscous. Turn off the heat, cover, and let stand for 10 minutes to absorb the stock. Taste, adjust the seasonings, and serve with the lamb.

Serves 6–8

NUTRIENT ANALYSIS PER SERVING 988 cal – 4108 kJ – 60 g protein – 52 g carbohydrate – 9 g sugars – 61 g fat – 26 g saturates – 1 g fiber – 0.4 g sodium

HEALTHY TIP A great dish, rich in protein, iron, zinc, and phosphorus.

Tangia, lamb shanks, and cumin

Tangia is the name of the earthenware pot in which the lamb in this dish is cooked. Normally, the tangia is buried in the ashes of a fire and left to cook all night. Chicken or rabbit are also cooked in the same way, the latter being very popular. Tangia of Marrakeshis, the dish par excellence, is a specialty prepared by men only, but in Fez, Tangia is prepared by the Fassiates women. They cook it in a *gamelle* (pan) and use veal oxtail to which saffron and paprika are added along with cumin and unpeeled garlic. Traditionally, this delicacy is eaten only with bread. For this recipe I put the dish on two heat diffusers over low heat so that the water is barely moving and the meat cooks very slowly. Four hours later the meat will be very tender and the smell very appetizing, but if left for another hour, melts completely, with only a little moisture remaining.

INGREDIENTS *4 lamb shanks, about 3 lb* ‖ *2 tablespoons olive oil* ‖ *½–¾ teaspoon ground cumin* ‖ *1 bay leaf* ‖ *¾ teaspoon salt, or to taste* ‖ *1 cup water* ‖ *4 garlic cloves, unpeeled*

ONE Put all the ingredients in a pan and put on a heat diffuser, if you have one, over low heat. Cover and let simmer for 4–5 hours, turning the lamb shanks gently 2–3 times, or until the meat is nearly falling off the bone. Discard bay leaf. **TWO** Serve on its own, with bread, roasted potatoes, or a salad (*see below*).

Serves 4

NUTRIENT ANALYSIS PER SERVING 484 cal – 2016 kJ – 50 g protein – 0 g carbohydrate – 0 g sugars – 31 g fat – 12 g saturates – 0 g fiber – 0.7 g sodium (if using 1¼ teaspoons salt)

HEALTHY TIP This dish is extremely rich in A and B vitamins, iron, zinc, potassium, magnesium, selenium, and germanium. Eat it with a rich antioxidant salad such as Grated Carrot and Orange Salad (*see page 34*) or Potato, Turmeric, and Cumin Salad (*see page 43*).

Lemony lamb and rice

This is a soothing, comforting dish. The meat and onions slowly release their juices, which mellow with the saffron. A touch of parsley and cilantro is thrown in along with a sprinkling of lemon juice, which brings out the herbs' full taste.

INGREDIENTS *1 lb boneless leg of lamb, cut into medium-sized chunks* ‖ *1½ teaspoons salt, divided, or to taste* ‖ *2½ cups water* ‖ *pinch saffron threads* ‖ *½ medium onion, grated* ‖ *1 lemon quarter* ‖ *½ tablespoon finely ground almonds* ‖ *2 tablespoons finely chopped parsley* ‖ *1 tablespoon finely chopped cilantro leaves* ‖ *1 tomato, peeled, seeded, and finely chopped* ‖ *½ tablespoon lemon juice* ‖ *pinch black pepper* ‖ *1 cup basmati rice, rinsed once and drained*

ONE Sprinkle the lamb with 1 teaspoon of the salt, place in a small pan, and let rest for a few minutes. Add the water and bring slowly to a boil, skimming the surface as foam forms. Add the saffron, onions, and lemon and return to a boil; reduce heat to low, cover, and simmer for 1 hour or until meat is tender. About 15 minutes before the end of cooking time, add the almonds, parsley, cilantro, and tomato. Toward the end of cooking time, stir in the lemon juice and sprinkle with the pepper. **TWO** Ladle 2 cups of the stock into a small pan and add the rice and remaining salt. Bring to a boil, then reduce heat to low, cover, and simmer for 8 minutes or until the stock is fully absorbed. **THREE** Transfer the rice to a serving dish and serve with the meat.

Serves 4–6

NUTRIENT ANALYSIS PER SERVING 420 cal – 1764 kJ – 30 g protein – 43 g carbohydrate – 3 g sugars – 14 g fat – 5 g saturates – 1 g fiber – 0.9 g sodium (if using 1½ teaspoons salt)

HEALTHY TIP This dish is nutritionally sound and is a rich source of good protein, B vitamins, iron, zinc, and phosphates.

Shreds of lamb in pomegranate juice

This dish will delight meat lovers with its rich flavor and speedy preparation. In Arabic it's known as *Shahm* ("fat"), because lamb in the Middle East usually has a tail full of fat that melts easily (although that's not the case in the West). My alterations to Ibn Razin el-Tujibi's recipe cut down the saturated fat in the dish. The recipe is said to be prepared in the north of Morocco, particularly in Tetouan. I have added the juice of a whole sour pomegranate, following the option he gave in the book. Additionally, I have added pomegranate syrup, which is also optional. Accompany this dish with Three Pepper Salad (*see page 48*) and Cucumber and Nut Salad (*see page 38*).

INGREDIENTS *1½ lb boneless lamb (leg or shoulder), cut into thin short strips* ‖ *1 teaspoon salt, or to taste* ‖ *1½ tablespoons extra virgin olive oil* ‖ *½ teaspoon black pepper* ‖ *½–¾ teaspoon ground caraway* ‖ *½–¾ teaspoon ground coriander* ‖ *1 tablespoon chopped cilantro leaves* ‖ *juice of 1 sour pomegranate, if available* ‖ *1 teaspoon lemon juice, if necessary* ‖ *½ tablespoon pomegranate syrup (optional)*

ONE Put the meat in a shallow nonstick skillet, season with the salt, and cook over medium-low heat for 1 minute. Add the oil and continue cooking, stirring occasionally, for about 8 minutes, or until thoroughly browned. Cover and let simmer for about 20 minutes, stirring from time to time, or until the liquid has evaporated. Taste a piece to check if it's done. Since the meat is thinly sliced, if it is of good quality it does not need water to tenderize it. **TWO** When the meat is tender, season with pepper, caraway, coriander, and cilantro, then stir well and cook for 1–2 minutes until the meat has browned and is nearly dry. Add the pomegranate juice, if using, and the lemon juice (if the pomegranate is not sour enough) and stir until the juices are absorbed by the meat. Taste and add the pomegranate syrup, if using. **THREE** Serve immediately with roasted potatoes or fries and salads (*see above*).

Serves 3–4

NUTRIENT ANALYSIS PER SERVING 480 cal – 2008 kJ – 53 g protein – 2 g carbohydrate – 2 g sugars – 29 g fat – 12 g saturates – 3 g fiber – 0.9 g sodium (if using 1 teaspoon salt)

HEALTHY TIP This dish is an excellent source of protein, B vitamins, iron, phosphorus, potassium, and zinc.

Lamb with tomatoes and onions

What a glorious tagine, known in Morocco as *Maqfoul,* meaning "locked." My knowledgeable guide Siddik told me that a good tagine needs to simmer on the stove for at least 2½ hours—the slower, the tastier. Following this advice, toward the end of the simmering I sprinkled the dish lightly with confectioners' sugar and finished cooking it in the oven.

INGREDIENTS *1½ lb boneless lamb (leg or shoulder), cut into medium-sized pieces* ‖ *1 teaspoon salt, or to taste* ‖ *½ cup water* ‖ *pinch saffron threads* ‖ *3 garlic cloves, crushed* ‖ *½ teaspoon ground cinnamon, divided* ‖ *1 lb onions, each cut into quarters* ‖ *1¼ tablespoons extra virgin olive oil, divided* ‖ *about 2 lb tomatoes, peeled, cut horizontally, and seeded* ‖ *½ teaspoon turmeric* ‖ *pinch freshly grated ginger root* ‖ *good pinch black pepper* ‖ *1 teaspoon confectioners' sugar (optional)*

ONE Tightly pack the meat together in a single layer in a medium ovenproof pan. Sprinkle all over with the salt and let stand for 5 minutes. Add the water and bring slowly to a boil, skimming the surface as foam forms, then add the saffron, garlic, half the cinnamon, and the onions, spreading them evenly over the meat. Drizzle all over with half the oil, then cover and simmer over very low heat for 30 minutes. If necessary, place a heat diffuser under the pan. **TWO** Put the tomatoes, cut side down, over the onions. Cover and simmer over low heat for 1 hour. **THREE** Check the amount of liquid in the pan and, if necessary, drain some off (reserve to use in soups), then add the turmeric, ginger, and pepper. Gently shake the pan to distribute the spices evenly, then sprinkle all over with the remaining cinnamon and oil and the confectioners' sugar, if using. Cover again and transfer to a preheated oven, 350°F, for 20–30 minutes. Uncover the pan and cook for 5 more minutes, then remove from oven and serve.

Serves 4–5

NUTRIENT ANALYSIS PER SERVING 440 cal – 1847 kJ – 43 g protein – 21 g carbohydrate – 18 g sugars – 21 g fat – 9 g saturates – 6 g fiber – 0.7 g sodium (if using 1 teaspoon salt)

HEALTHY TIP *Maqfoul* has valuable nutrients that fight the free radicals that destroy healthy cells. It supplies A and B vitamins, phosphorus, magnesium, potassium, iron, zinc, quercetin, selenium, and sulfur.

Tagine of lamb and eggplant

During my stay in Fez, Madame Sefraoui suggested this dish. It was so delicious that I couldn't wait to prepare it at home. Rather than frying the eggplants, you can slice them into rounds, brush with oil, and broil or grill to brown on both sides.

INGREDIENTS *1¼ lb eggplant, sliced lengthwise into ¾ inch widths* ‖ *salt* ‖ *1 lb boneless lamb (shoulder or leg), cut into 4–8 equal pieces* ‖ *extra virgin olive oil, as needed* ‖ *pinch saffron threads* ‖ *½ teaspoon ground ginger* ‖ *¼ teaspoon ground coriander* ‖ *4–8 tablepoons water* ‖ *2 lb tomatoes, peeled, seeded, and coarsely chopped* ‖ *2 garlic cloves, finely crushed* ‖ *¾ teaspoon paprika* ‖ *½ teaspoon turmeric* ‖ *¾ teaspoon ground cumin* ‖ *1 tablespoon finely chopped cilantro leaves* ‖ *1 tablespoon finely chopped parsley* ‖ *½ teaspoon sugar* ‖ *¾–1 tablespoon lemon juice*

ONE If the eggplant slices are very large, salt them all over, place in a colander over a bowl, and let stand for 1–2 hours to drain. **TWO** Meanwhile, rub the lamb with ½ teaspoon salt and place in a small to medium pan and let stand for 5 minutes. Add ½ teaspoon oil to the meat, place over medium heat, and stir for about 1 minute, then add the saffron, ginger, and coriander and stir well. Add 4 tablespoons of the water, reduce heat to very low, cover, and simmer for about 1 hour or until the meat is very tender. Check the water level from time to time—you may need to add another 3–4 tablespoons water. **THREE** Meanwhile, put the tomatoes, garlic, and a pinch of salt in a small skillet, place over medium heat, and simmer for 1–2 minutes, then add the paprika. Continue cooking until nearly all the juices have evaporated, then stir in the turmeric, cumin, 1 teaspoon oil, cilantro, parsley, and sugar; cook until it reaches a thick consistency. **FOUR** Rinse the eggplant slices very well, gently squeeze out the excess water, and dry the slices between paper towels. Heat some oil until hot but not smoking, then fry the eggplant slices on both sides until brown. Remove and drain well on several changes of paper towels. Let cool to room temperature, then drizzle with lemon juice; using a fork, gently mash to mix the slices thoroughly with the juice. **FIVE** Place the eggplant slices on the meat, top with the tomato mixture, cover, and simmer for 10 minutes. **SIX** Shake the pan, but do not stir. Serve with bread.

Serves 4–5

NUTRIENT ANALYSIS PER SERVING 298 cal – 1252 kJ – 29 g protein – 12 g carbohydrate – 12 g sugars – 15 g fat – 6 g saturates – 7 g fiber – 0.4 g sodium

HEALTHY TIP This is rich in antioxidants and the body-building blocks, protein and in the B vitamins, iron and zinc.

Tagine of lamb, quince, and honey

Here is a delicious dish. The marriage of fruits, meat, and spices is sensual and exciting to work with, mouth-watering and addictive. The spices produce a wonderful aroma, while the quinces have substances that help break down the fat and meat.

INGREDIENTS *½ tablespoon extra virgin olive oil* ‖ *1 lb boneless lamb (leg or shoulder), cut into medium-sized pieces, fat trimmed* ‖ *2 cups water* ‖ *½ teaspoon salt* ‖ *¼ teaspoon black pepper* ‖ *½ teaspoon saffron threads* ‖ *2 cinnamon sticks* ‖ *1 bay leaf* ‖ *2 cloves* ‖ *1 celery stick, cut into 3 pieces* ‖ *1–2 quinces, unpeeled, each quartered and seeded* ‖ *1 teaspoon brown sugar* ‖ *¾ teaspoon ground cinnamon* ‖ *½ tablespoon honey*

ONE Heat a pan, add the oil and lamb, and sauté over medium-high heat for a few minutes to brown the meat on all sides. Add the water and bring slowly to a boil, skimming the surface as foam forms. Season with the salt, pepper, and saffron and add the cinnamon sticks, bay leaf, cloves, and celery. Return to a boil, reduce heat to medium-low, cover, and simmer for 30 minutes. **TWO** Add the quince pieces and return to a boil; reduce heat, cover, and cook for 30 minutes or until the meat and quinces are tender. At this stage, if desired, the quinces can be carefully removed from the pan and placed under a hot broiler to brown, then returned to the pan to finish cooking. **THREE** Sprinkle with the sugar, ground cinnamon, and honey and cook for another 10–15 minutes. Discard cinnamon sticks and bay leaf. Taste, adjust seasonings, and serve with couscous or bulgar.

Serves 4

NUTRIENT ANALYSIS PER SERVING 242 cal – 1017 kJ – 26 g protein – 7 g carbohydrate – 7 g sugars – 13g fat – 6 g saturates – 2 g fiber – 0.4 g sodium

HEALTHY TIP This dish is rich in protein, iron, zinc, B vitamins, and fiber.

Lamb tagine with carrots

The famous tagines of Morocco can be made with a variety of vegetables, including carrots, and this healthy tagine has a lovely taste. As I was going through a 13th-century cook book I fell for its title *"al-Nargissia"* (The Narcissus).

INGREDIENTS *1 lb boneless lamb (leg or shoulder), cut into medium-sized pieces* ‖ *1 teaspoon salt* ‖ *2½ cups water* ‖ *1 lb carrots, peeled and cut into 2 inch sticks* ‖ *2 garlic cloves, crushed* ‖ *2 teaspoons extra virgin olive oil* ‖ *1 teaspoon turmeric* ‖ *good pinch freshly grated ginger root* ‖ *handful finely chopped cilantro leaves*

RICE *1 cup basmati rice, rinsed once and drained* ‖ *⅔ cup water* ‖ *½ teaspoon salt*

ONE Rub the lamb with the salt, place in a pan, and let stand for 5 minutes. Add the water and bring slowly to a boil, skimming the surface as foam forms. Reduce heat to low, cover, and simmer for about 50 minutes. **TWO** Add the carrots, garlic, and oil, then cover and simmer for 10–15 minutes. **THREE** Add the turmeric, ginger, and cilantro and cook for 5 minutes; remove from heat. **FOUR** Put the rice in a small pan and add 1¼ cups of the stock from the tagine, the water, and salt. Bring to a boil over medium heat, reduce heat to very low, cover, and simmer gently for 8–10 minutes until the liquid is absorbed. **FIVE** Serve the lamb and carrot tagine with the rice, and some bread if desired.

Serves 4

NUTRIENT ANALYSIS PER SERVING 452 cal – 1890 kJ – 30 g protein – 50 g carbohydrate – 9 g sugars – 14 g fat – 6 g saturates – 3 g fiber – 0.9 g sodium (if using 1½ teaspoons salt)

HEALTHY TIP This dish is a valuable source of B vitamins, important for the functioning of the nervous system, for energy, and reinforcing the immune system. It is also high in betacarotene, a powerful antioxidant that combats many illnesses, and is rich in potassium, phosphorus, selenium, boron, and iron.

Fish

Fish in aromatic sauce

A lovely, generous Moroccan lady, Madame Lazrak, recommended this dish to me. It is prepared with Chermoula Sauce, an aromatic mixture of powerful herbs and spices that is smeared over the fish, making the fish not only more palatable, but protecting its health-giving oils. The sauce can be used with any kind of fish.

INGREDIENTS *2 lb sea bass or hake, gutted and scaled* ‖ *1 teaspoon salt, or to taste* ‖ *1 lb potatoes, thinly sliced* ‖ *1 lb tomatoes, each cut into 3 slices* ‖ *1 recipe Chermoula Sauce (see page 14)* ‖ *1 green or red bell pepper, cored, seeded, and cut into 2–3 slices* ‖ *2 whole chilies* ‖ *3 tablespoons extra virgin olive oil*

ONE Wash the fish with cold water and pat dry. Sprinkle inside and out with ½ teaspoon of the salt. Mix the potatoes and tomatoes together with the remaining salt and about 1 tablespoon of the Chermoula Sauce. **TWO** Make a bed of potatoes in a baking pan. Rub the fish inside and out with the remaining Chermoula Sauce and place it on top of the potatoes. **THREE** Arrange the tomatoes, sliced peppers, and chilies around and on top of the fish. Drizzle with the oil and bake in a preheated oven, 350°F, for 30–40 minutes, basting twice. Remove from the oven and serve.

Serves 4

NUTRIENT ANALYSIS PER SERVING 1925 kJ – 460 cal – 41 g protein – 82 g carbohydrate – 5 g sugars – 20 g fat – 2 g saturates – 4 g fiber – 1.1 g sodium (if using 1 teaspoon salt)

HEALTHY TIP Consuming fish is highly beneficial and eating it twice a week is recommended. It contains omega-3 fatty acids, which have numerous benefits—they protect the arteries and fortify the heart muscles, which, in turn, regulate the heart rate. It also increases the amount of good cholesterol and may help prevent some cancers. Some fish are more abundant than others in omega-3 fatty acids, notably sardines, mackerel, salmon, tuna, and herring.

B'steeya of fish

I got this recipe during my stay in Essaouira, on the Atlantic coast, which was a Phoenician staging post in earlier times. It is easy to prepare and will appeal even to children who do not like fish.

INGREDIENTS *2 lb sea bass, gutted and scaled* ‖ *1½ teaspoons ground cumin* ‖ *pinch salt* ‖ *1 tablespoon extra virgin olive oil, divided* ‖ *3 sheets filo pastry* ‖ *1 egg yolk*

RICE *¾ cup basmati rice, rinsed once and drained* ‖ *1¼ cups water* ‖ *½ teaspoon salt* ‖ *2 tablespoons extra virgin olive oil* ‖ *5–6 heaping tablespoons chopped cilantro leaves*

ONE Steam the fish over boiling water for 8–10 minutes, or brush with oil and bake in a preheated oven, 350°F, for 18–20 minutes. Remove and, when cool enough to handle, discard the skin and bones. Put the fish in a bowl, sprinkle with cumin, salt, and ½ tablespoon of the oil, and stir to mix thoroughly. Divide into 4 equal portions. **TWO** Put the rice, water, and salt in a heavy pan. Bring to a boil, reduce heat to low, cover, and simmer for 6–8 minutes or until the water has been absorbed. Add the oil and stir to mix with the rice, then add the cilantro and mix thoroughly. Divide the rice into 4 equal portions. **THREE** Take 2 sheets of filo pastry and fold in half. Slice to get 4 equal sheets and place under a clean, damp kitchen towel. Fold the remaining sheet once and fold again and again until you end up with a square shape. Using a 5 inch diameter plate as a template, and with a pointed knife, slice around the plate to get neat filo rounds. **FOUR** To assemble, take one of the larger pastry sheets and place a smaller round in the middle, to strengthen the base. Spoon on one portion of rice and press lightly to form a circular shape. Place another pastry round on top of the rice. Spoon one portion of fish onto the round and press lightly as before. Brush the overhanging edges of the pastry with egg yolk and fold over the filling to form a round. Brush all over with a little of the remaining oil and egg yolk. Repeat with remaining ingredients to make 4 pies. **FIVE** Bake on the lower shelf of a preheated oven, 375°F, for 10–15 minutes or until golden brown.

Serves 4

NUTRIENT ANALYSIS PER SERVING 470 cal – 1970 kJ – 40 g protein – 44 g carbohydrate – 1 g sugars – 15 g fat – 2 g saturates – 0 g fiber – 0.5 g sodium

HEALTHY TIP Consuming fish protects the heart and brain cells and sharpens alertness. This dish is rich in E and B vitamins, potassium, and phosphorus (important for heart muscle contraction).

Sardines in aromatic herbs
This way of cooking sardines reduces their strong flavor.

INGREDIENTS *10 oz sardine fillets* ‖ *2 large garlic cloves, crushed* ‖ *1 small slice onion, grated* ‖ *½ cup cilantro leaves* ‖ *1¼ teaspoons ground cumin, divided* ‖ *scant ½ teaspoon black pepper* ‖ *½ teaspoon turmeric, divided* ‖ *1¼ teaspoons salt, divided or to taste* ‖ *1 tablespoon extra virgin olive oil* ‖ *6 oz onions, sliced* ‖ *a few saffron threads* ‖ *¾ tablespoon tomato paste* ‖ *2 large tomatoes, peeled, seeded and finely chopped* ‖ *½ red bell pepper, cored, seeded, and sliced into thin strips* ‖ *⅔ cup water* ‖ *handful finely chopped parsley* ‖ *handful finely chopped cilantro leaves* ‖ *2–3 small chilies, halved and seeded* ‖ *handful fresh or frozen peas* ‖ *1½ tablespoons lemon juice, or to taste*

ONE Put the sardines, garlic, grated onion, measured cilantro, ¾ teaspoon of the cumin, the pepper, ¼ teaspoon of the turmeric, and ¾ teaspoon of the salt in a food processor and blend until smooth. Pour the mixture into a bowl and, working with moist hands, form into 16 balls slightly smaller than walnuts. Set aside. **TWO** Heat a pan, add the oil, and, when hot, add the sliced onions and sauté until translucent and yellowish in color. Add the saffron, tomato paste, tomatoes, red pepper, and water and bring to a boil; reduce heat to medium-low and simmer for a few minutes. **THREE** Add the sardine balls to the pan, sprinkle with the handfuls of parsley and cilantro, then add the chilies, peas, and the remaining cumin, turmeric, and salt. Cover and simmer for 8–10 minutes. **FOUR** Sprinkle with lemon juice and adjust the seasonings, then serve with barley semolina, couscous, or rice.

Serves 3–4

NUTRIENT ANALYSIS PER SERVING 269 cal – 1125 kJ – 24 g protein – 13 g carbohydrate – 10 g sugars – 14 g fat – 3 g saturates – 4 g fiber – 1 g sodium

HEALTHY TIP Sardines are an excellent source of omega-3 fatty acids, which increase good HDL cholesterol in the body, reduce cardiovascular disease, boost immunity to prevent many cancers, and nourish and rejuvenate cells in the brain and body. The fish are also high in zinc, which protects from prostate cancer. This is a nutritious dish rich in vitamin D, the antioxidant lycopene, germanium, sulfur, selenium, and co-enzyme Q-10, which is said to combat obesity, diabetes, and much more.

Jumbo shrimp M'chermel in tomato sauce The ingredients of this dish typify the healthy Mediterranean diet!

INGREDIENTS *2 tablespoons finely chopped cilantro leaves* ‖ *1 tablespoon finely chopped parsley* ‖ *2 garlic cloves* ‖ *pinch paprika* ‖ *pinch ground cumin* ‖ *1 teaspoon salt, divided, or to taste* ‖ *1 tablespoon extra virgin olive oil, divided* ‖ *½–1 tablespoon lemon juice, divided* ‖ *16 jumbo shrimp, peeled* ‖ *½ medium onion, finely chopped* ‖ *¼–½ teaspoon turmeric* ‖ *1½ lb tomatoes, peeled, seeded, and chopped*

ONE Put the cilantro, parsley, garlic, paprika, cumin, and ½ teaspoon of the salt in a mortar and pound with a pestle until creamy. Gradually add ½ tablespoon of the oil and ½ tablespoon of the lemon juice. Rub this sauce into the jumbo shrimp, cover, and refrigerate for at least 1 hour. **TWO** About 30 minutes before serving, prepare the tomato sauce. Heat a skillet and add the remaining oil, the onions, turmeric, and tomatoes, sprinkle with the remaining salt and simmer over medium-low heat for about 8 minutes. **THREE** Add the jumbo shrimp and cook for about 4 minutes, until they turn pink in color. Taste, add the remaining lemon juice if necessary, and serve hot.

Serves 4

NUTRIENT ANALYSIS PER SERVING 108 cal – 454 kJ – 9 g protein – 9 g carbohydrate – 8 g sugars – 4 g fat – 1 g saturates – 3 g fiber – 1 g sodium (if using 1 teaspoon salt)

HEALTHY TIP This dish is rich in amino acids, omega-3 fatty acids, phosphorus, antioxidants, B vitamins, selenium, and zinc and is an excellent food for the brain, memory, intellect, and beauty.

Fish with pumpkin and aromatic herbs

This fish dish is prepared with carrots, pumpkin, olives, and aromatic herbs—an astonishing combination maybe, but it still works extremely well and is delectable. The pumpkin and carrots are not precooked, but, if desired, steaming or sautéeing them for a short while before adding to the stuffing cuts down on the baking time. Marinate the fish in the morning and cook it in the evening for a better flavor.

INGREDIENTS *2 lb sea bass with head, gutted and scaled* ‖ *1½ teaspoons salt, divided* ‖ *4 oz peeled pumpkin, seeded and coarsely grated* ‖ *2 medium carrots, coarsely grated* ‖ *2 garlic cloves, crushed* ‖ *about ½ teaspoon freshly grated ginger root* ‖ *¼ teaspoon black pepper* ‖ *12 black olives, pitted, rinsed, and coarsely chopped* ‖ *½ teaspoon turmeric* ‖ *½ teaspoon cumin* ‖ *2 tablespoons finely chopped cilantro leaves* ‖ *1 heaping tablespoon finely chopped parsley* ‖ *¼–½ teaspoon paprika* ‖ *1 teaspoon organic apple cider vinegar* ‖ *2–3 tablespoons extra virgin olive oil, divided* ‖ *1 slice preserved lemon (see page 13), rinsed, pulp discarded, and rind cut into small pieces (optional)* ‖ *2 tablespoons lemon juice*

ONE Wash the fish with cold water, pat dry and score 2 diagonal cuts on each side. Rub the fish inside and out with ½ teaspoon of the salt. **TWO** Put the pumpkin and carrots in a bowl, add the garlic, the remaining salt, the ginger, pepper, olives, turmeric, cumin, cilantro, parsley, paprika, vinegar, 1½ tablespoons of the oil, the preserved lemon rind (if using), and lemon juice and mix thoroughly. **THREE** Stuff the fish cavity with the mixture, spread the remainder over the fish, and put in a roasting pan. Drizzle with the remaining oil, ensuring that it is coated on all sides so that the fish does not stick to the pan. Cover and refrigerate for at least 1–2 hours to allow the fish to absorb the seasonings. **FOUR** Bake the fish in a preheated oven, 350°F, for 30–40 minutes.

Serves 4

NUTRIENT ANALYSIS PER SERVING 264 cal – 1106 kJ – 35 g protein – 4 g carbohydrate – 3 g sugars – 12 g fat – 2 g saturates – 2 g fiber – 1.3 g sodium

HEALTHY TIP This dish is highly valuable as an excellent source of protein, betacarotene, vitamin C, and selenium.

Fish tagine with couscous
In Morocco, this unusual tagine is prepared with conger eel.

INGREDIENTS *2 lb sea bass with head, gutted and scaled* ‖ *1½ teaspoons salt, divided* ‖ *1 small onion, peeled and studded with 2 cloves* ‖ *5 stems parsley with leaves* ‖ *3 stems cilantro with leaves* ‖ *1 large cinnamon stick* ‖ *2 bay leaves* ‖ *7½ cups water* ‖ *1¾ tablespoons extra virgin olive oil, divided* ‖ *good pinch saffron threads* ‖ *¼–½ teaspoon black pepper* ‖ *½ teaspoon turmeric* ‖ *1 lb red onions, sliced* ‖ *2 garlic cloves* ‖ *¼ cup raisins* ‖ *¼ cup golden raisins* ‖ *¼ teaspoon ground cinnamon* ‖ *good pinch freshly grated ginger root* ‖ *½ tablespoon honey*

COUSCOUS *1¾ cups fine organic couscous* ‖ *1 teaspoon salt* ‖ *1 tablespoon extra virgin olive oil*

ONE Rinse the fish, pat dry, and sprinkle inside and out with ½ teaspoon of the salt. Cut off the head and trim the tail trimmings; discard tails. Slice the fish into 3 pieces. Put the clove-studded onion, parsley, cilantro, cinnamon stick, and bay leaves in a pan and place the head and fish pieces on top. Add the water and bring slowly to a boil, skimming the surface as foam forms. Add ¼ tablespoon of the oil and the saffron. Reduce heat and simmer gently for 5 minutes. **TWO** Remove the fish pieces, but leave the fish head and simmer for 40–50 minutes. Add the pepper and turmeric and cook for 10 minutes. **THREE** Meanwhile, gently sauté the red onions in the remaining oil until translucent. Stir in the garlic and cook briefly, then add 1¼ cups of the stock. Simmer gently for 15 minutes. Add the raisins and cook until the red onions are soft. Add the ground cinnamon, ginger, and honey, increase heat, and simmer for a few minutes to caramelize the red onions. **FOUR** Meanwhile, cover the couscous with water, rake it through with your fingers, then drain and immediately spread it evenly over a large tray or shallow pan. Rake the grains with your fingers a few times to aerate them, then leave for 20–30 minutes until the water is absorbed and the couscous is relatively dry. Sprinkle with the remaining salt and rub the grains between your palms to free them of any lumps. Place in the top of a couscoussière over boiling water (or in a fine steamer) and steam for 15 minutes. Transfer to a dish, sprinkle with the oil and mix gently to break up any lumps. Add about 1¼ cups of the stock and stir to combine. **FIVE** Serve the couscous topped with the fish and caramelized onions.

Serves 4–6

NUTRIENT ANALYSIS PER SERVING 600 cal – 2527 kJ – 42 g protein – 83 g carbohydrate – 32 g sugars – 14 g fat – 2 g saturates – 4 g fiber – 1.3 g sodium

HEALTHY TIP Eating fish regularly keeps you healthy through old age and also helps reduce wrinkles.

Vegetables

Mallow, aromatic herbs, and olives

Mallow is a plant that grows in the Mediterranean, Middle East, and many other parts of the world. In Morocco it is known as *Bekkoula*, in Lebanon as *Khobeiza*, and in France as *Mauve*. The leaves contain a gelatinous substance that is antibacterial and antiinflammatory. My grandmother treated skin conditions by wrapping them with mallow leaves, which were left until the condition cleared. She even boiled the leaves with water to be drunk for a sore throat or for any other inflammatory ailments. If mallow is not available, use spinach. Eat with grilled chicken or fish.

INGREDIENTS *1 lb mallow leaves or spinach* ‖ *about 3 cups parsley* ‖ *about 2½ cups cilantro stems with leaves* ‖ *3 garlic cloves, unpeeled* ‖ *4 oz celery leaves, finely chopped* ‖ *1 teaspoon salt, or to taste* ‖ *2 tablespoons extra virgin olive oil* ‖ *¼ cup lemon juice* ‖ *juice of 1 small orange* ‖ *1 teaspoon paprika* ‖ *a few small slices preserved lemon (see page 13) or fresh lemon* ‖ *10–12 halved purple or black olives, rinsed well* ‖ *pinch cayenne pepper, or to taste* ‖ *pomegranate seeds or 1 tablespoon pomegranate syrup (optional)* ‖ *black pepper*

ONE Gather the mallow or spinach leaves in a bunch and slice finely, including any tender stems. Discard the parsley and cilantro stems, gather the leaves in a bunch, and chop finely. **TWO** Place the mallow or spinach and garlic in a pan over very low heat; place the remaining ingredients in a salad bowl. **THREE** When the greens have reduced in size, turn off the heat and remove the garlic. Discard the skin, then cream the garlic and add to the ingredients in the bowl. Let the mallow mixture cool for 5 minutes, then add to the bowl and toss. Taste and adjust the seasonings.

VARIATION: Steam the mallow, garlic, and celery only. When ready, cream the garlic and cool the mallow and celery. Add the parsley and cilantro and toss with the remaining ingredients.

Serves 4–6

NUTRIENT ANALYSIS PER SERVING 129 cal – 533 kJ – 6 g protein – 6 g carbohydrate – 5 g sugars – 9 g fat – 1 g saturates – 10 g fiber – 1 g sodium (if using 1 teaspoon salt)

HEALTHY TIP This dish is a blood purifier that lowers bad (LDL) cholesterol. It contains a good amount of C and E vitamins, both powerful antioxidants that neutralize free radicals in the body. It is also rich in iron, magnesium, calcium, and phosphorus. Mallow and the aromatic herbs are palate fresheners, diuretic, and may prevent cancer.

Peppers with tomatoes

Here is one of the many delicious Moroccan appetizers of cooked vegetables. It's simple to make and marries well with meat, chicken, and fish dishes. For vegetarians, eat with couscous or quinoa, which is rich in protein. For those who don't like spicy foods, use a mild chili pepper instead.

INGREDIENTS *3 green bell peppers* ‖ *1 chili pepper* ‖ *1½ lb tomatoes* ‖ *1½–2 tablespoons extra virgin olive oil, divided* ‖ *½–1 teaspoon paprika* ‖ *1 large garlic clove, crushed* ‖ *1 teaspoon tomato paste (optional)* ‖ *1 teaspoon salt, or to taste* ‖ *3 heaping tablespoons finely chopped cilantro leaves* ‖ *2 heaping tablespoons finely chopped parsley* ‖ *pinch black pepper (optional)*

ONE Place the bell peppers and chili on a heat diffuser over a medium gas flame. Turn them for 3–5 minutes to char all over—the chili needs much less time, so keep an eye on it. Alternatively, preheat the broiler to high, then broil the peppers for 18 minutes or until charred on all sides. **TWO** Meanwhile, peel, seed, and finely cube the tomatoes. Heat a medium to large shallow pan, add 1 tablespoon of the oil, the paprika, garlic, tomato paste, if using, and tomatoes; sprinkle with the salt. Stir well and cook for 20 minutes or until the water has evaporated (some tomatoes have more water than others). **THREE** When the peppers and chili are cool enough to handle, peel and seed them, then cut into cubes. Add to the tomatoes with the cilantro and parsley, stir in the remaining oil, and cook for 5 more minutes. Sprinkle with the pepper, if using, and serve warm or at room temperature.

Serves 4–6

NUTRIENT ANALYSIS PER SERVING 109 cal – 454 kJ – 4 g protein – 8 g carbohydrate – 7 g sugars – 7 g fat – 1 g saturates – 9 g fiber – 0.5 g sodium (if using 1 teaspoon salt)

HEALTHY TIP This dish is loaded with vitamins E and C and the potent antioxidant lycopene, which may prevent prostate cancer. Chilies have long been used in pharmaceutical preparations, and creams are made from them to calm and relieve rheumatism and arthritis. They help the circulation and are anticancerous and antiseptic.

Pulses, grains, and barley couscous A complex carbohydrate dish called *Urkimen*.

INGREDIENTS *⅓ cup dried chickpeas, soaked overnight* ‖ *⅓ cup dried fava beans, soaked overnight* ‖ *¼ cup dried corn or maize, soaked overnight* ‖ *7½–8½ cups water* ‖ *¼ cup dried navy beans, soaked 6 hours* ‖ *⅓ cup brown lentils* ‖ *¼ cup dried peas* ‖ *1 lb onions, sliced* ‖ *¼ cup coarse bulgar* ‖ *2 large tomatoes, peeled and diced* ‖ *1 medium eggplant, cut into chunks* ‖ *8 oz carrots, cut into thick sticks* ‖ *1 large turnip, cut into thick sticks* ‖ *2½ tablespoons extra virgin olive oil, divided* ‖ *2 zucchini, cubed* ‖ *2½ teaspoons paprika* ‖ *½–¾ teaspoon black pepper* ‖ *2½ cups barley semolina couscous (belboula)* ‖ *salt*

ONE Put the drained, rinsed chickpeas, fava beans, and corn in the bottom of a couscoussière or pan with the measured water. Bring slowly to a boil, skimming the surface. Cover and simmer gently for 1 hour. **TWO** Add the drained, rinsed navy beans, lentils, and peas to the pan. Skim again and add the onions. Bring to a boil, reduce heat, cover, and simmer for 5–10 minutes. Add the bulgar, tomatoes, and eggplant and simmer for 5–10 minutes. **THREE** Add the carrots, turnip, and 1½ tablespoons of the oil and cook for 10 minutes. Add the zucchini and hot water, if necessary, and simmer for 5–10 minutes until all the ingredients are tender. Sprinkle with salt to taste, the paprika, and pepper. **FOUR** Cover the couscous with water. Rake it through with your fingers, then drain and immediately spread it evenly over a large tray or shallow pan. Rake the grains with your fingers a few times to aerate them, then leave for 20–30 minutes until the water is absorbed and the couscous is relatively dry. Rub the couscous gently between your palms, allowing it to fall back into the tray or pan, to break down any lumps. Place in the top of the couscoussière or meshed strainer over the grains and legumes and steam for 30 minutes, separating the grains twice with a fork. **FIVE** Remove and spread over a large tray, sprinkle with some water and 1 teaspoon salt, and aerate and separate the grains as before. Let stand until the water is absorbed, then sprinkle with 1½ teaspoons salt, and gently rub the grains. Steam for another 30 minutes. **SIX** Remove and spread over a large tray, sprinkle with the remaining oil and a ladleful of stock, then mix, separate the grains, and let stand to absorb the water. Rub and then steam again for 15 minutes. **SEVEN** Serve with the grains and legumes.

Serves 8

NUTRIENT ANALYSIS PER SERVING 392 cal – 1645 kJ – 16 g protein – 70 g carbohydrate – 9 g sugars – 6 g fat – 1 g saturates – 7 g fiber – 0.6 g sodium (if using 2½ teaspoons salt)

HEALTHY TIP Rich in fiber, vitamins E and B, magnesium, selenium, potassium, chromium, zinc, iron, and molybdenum.

Eggplant & pepper ratatouille

In this Moroccan dish, I don't use water and I cook the vegetables for a short period of time to preserve their nutrients. The tomatoes are peeled to be in harmony with the texture of the other vegetables, but you can keep the peel on, if preferred, which helps to retain more of their soluble vitamins. The dish has a good balance of acidic and nonacidic ingredients. When barbecuing, prepare it in advance to serve with meat, fish, or chicken. Eat warm or at room temperature.

INGREDIENTS *2 large green or red bell peppers, or a mixture* ‖ *1 lb eggplants, cut into small cubes* ‖ *10 oz zucchini, cut into small cubes* ‖ *1¼ lb tomatoes, peeled, seeded, and cut into small cubes* ‖ *2 large garlic cloves, crushed* ‖ *1¼ teaspoons salt, or to taste* ‖ *1 teaspoon paprika* ‖ *pinch black pepper* ‖ *2 whole chilies* ‖ *1–2 tablespoons extra virgin olive or peanut oil* ‖ *pinch ground cumin (optional)*

ONE Preheat the broiler to high, then roast the peppers for 18 minutes or until charred on all sides. Alternatively, place the peppers on a heat diffuser over a medium gas flame. Turn them for 3–5 minutes to char all over. Let the peppers cool, then peel, seed, and cut the flesh into small cubes. Set aside. **TWO** Put the eggplant, zucchini, and tomatoes in a medium pan, stir in the garlic, and sprinkle with the salt, paprika, and pepper. Add the chilies and drizzle with the oil, then stir gently to help the vegetables release their liquid. Cover, place over medium heat, and simmer for 20 minutes, stirring gently 2–3 times during cooking. **THREE** Stir in the pepper cubes and cook for 1–2 minutes, then sprinkle with the cumin, if using. Serve warm or cold.

Serves 4–5

NUTRIENT ANALYSIS PER SERVING 139 cal – 585 kJ – 5 g protein – 15 g carbohydrate – 10 g sugars – 7 g fat – 1 g saturates – 6 g fiber – 0.6 g sodium (if using 1¼ teaspoons salt)

HEALTHY TIP Vegetables are indispensable for good health and are said to be anti-aging. They are low in fat, have a high water content, and are rich in fiber, which is important for good bowel function. When cooked, their fiber becomes easier to digest.

Marinated eggplants

When in season, baby eggplants adorn the shelves of farmers' markets and grocery stores. However, we wonder how to prepare them. This tasty Moroccan preparation—called *Aubergines m'Rekked*—answers the question. It is quick to make and ideal to serve with a drink when friends are around. Traditionally, the eggplants are boiled, but I prefer to steam them. Other vegetables may be used instead.

INGREDIENTS *1 lb baby eggplants* ‖ *5 garlic cloves* ‖ *3 tablespoons lemon juice* ‖ *¾ teaspoon ground cumin* ‖ *2–3 tablespoons finely chopped parsley* ‖ *¾ teaspoon sea salt* ‖ *1 teaspoon paprika* ‖ *1½ teaspoons ground coriander* ‖ *2 tablespoons extra virgin olive oil*

ONE Steam the eggplants and garlic for 6–8 minutes until slightly soft. Place in a colander and set aside to drain well. Cut the eggplants lengthwise into quarters to within ½ inch of the stem, leaving them attached at the end. **TWO** Peel the garlic, cream using a mortar and pestle, and mix thoroughly with the remaining ingredients. **THREE** Gently stuff some of this mixture into each eggplant. Put the stuffed eggplants in a clean jar, cover tightly and set aside for a few hours, then turn upside down. The eggplants will be ready to eat within 6 hours, but the flavors will slowly develop after 1–2 days.

Serves 6–8

NUTRIENT ANALYSIS PER SERVING 50 cal – 206 kJ – 1 g protein – 2 g carbohydrate – 2 g sugars – 4 g fat – 1 g saturates – 2 g fiber – 0.3 g sodium

HEALTHY TIP These marinated eggplants are very tasty and fight cancer, act as a diuretic, and may lower bad (LDL) cholesterol. They contain powerful antioxidants, vitamins E and C, selenium, and germanium. As well as adding flavor, garlic blocks the moderate gas found in eggplants.

Eggplant and potato cakes

Eggplants were introduced to Morocco by the Arabs. This magical vegetable enhances the flavor of whatever ingredient it is cooked with. The recipe in the book of Ibn Razine al-Tujibi, which is believed to have been written between 1238 and 1266, uses eggplant with ground lamb, but instead of lamb I opted for potatoes. Besides being nutritious, they are comforting and marry well with the eggplants. These cakes are delicious and crisp on the outside while remaining soft on the inside—children will like them, and they are suitable for vegetarians and people of all ages. You can also make miniature ones to serve at parties.

INGREDIENTS *1 lb eggplants, thickly sliced* ‖ *4 garlic cloves, unpeeled* ‖ *1 lb potatoes, scrubbed and left whole* ‖ *½ medium onion, grated* ‖ *¼ cup finely chopped cilantro leaves* ‖ *¾ teaspoon salt* ‖ *½ teaspoon ground cumin, or to taste* ‖ *pinch paprika* ‖ *1 egg white* ‖ *peanut oil, for greasing and frying*

ONE Steam the eggplant slices and garlic for 6–8 minutes. Remove the garlic and peel, then mash with the eggplant. **TWO** Steam the potatoes until cooked yet firm. Let cool, then grate coarsely, and mix with the eggplant, onion, cilantro, salt, cumin, and paprika. Beat the egg white, then fold into the eggplant and potato mixture and let stand for 5 minutes. Alternatively, to make shaping the cakes easier, put the mixture in the refrigerator for 5–10 minutes. **THREE** Oil your hands, then form the mixture into 1¼ inch rounds. Heat the oil in a frying pan until hot, then fry the cakes until golden all over. Alternatively, broil for 3–5 minutes on each side until lightly browned, although they won't be as crisp. Drain on a double layer of paper towels and eat hot or at room temperature. Serve with Orange, Black Olive, and Watercress Salad (*see page 51*).

Makes 14–16

NUTRIENT ANALYSIS PER SERVING 39 cal – 166 kJ – 1 g protein – 7 g carbohydrate – 1 g sugars – 1 g fat – 0 g saturates – 1 g fiber – 0.1 g sodium

HEALTHY TIP These cakes are rich in potassium, phosphorus, magnesium, amino acids, and vitamin C, which is lost if potatoes are boiled for a long time; steaming and baking are better options.

Cauliflower with spices

This is another lovely dish inspired by the 13th-century Moroccan cookbook of Ibn Razine al-Tujibi. Authentically, it is made with meat, but I have tried it without and found that it is light with a clean aftertaste. Serve with Briouats with Meat or with Shrimp and Sea Bass (*see pages 138 and 140*).

INGREDIENTS *1 tablespoon extra virgin olive oil* ‖ *¾ teaspoon ground coriander* ‖ *2 tablespoons cilantro leaves, finely chopped* ‖ *1 medium onion, sliced* ‖ *2½ lb cauliflower, broken into florets* ‖ *scant ⅔ cup water, or as needed* ‖ *2 teaspoons all-purpose flour* ‖ *good pinch freshly grated ginger root* ‖ *¼ teaspoon ground cumin* ‖ *2–3 tablespoons lemon juice*

ONE Heat the oil in a medium pan. Add the coriander and cilantro, onions, and cauliflower, stir well, and add the water. Bring to a boil, reduce heat to very low, cover, and simmer for 15–20 minutes. **TWO** Stir 1½ tablespoons of the cauliflower stock into the flour until smooth, then add to the cauliflower in the pan. Simmer for a few minutes, then season with the ginger, cumin, and lemon juice. Let stand for 1–2 minutes for the flavors to develop, then serve warm or at room temperature.

VARIATION: The cauliflower florets can be steamed and then added to all the other ingredients (except the flour and water) to be used as a salad. Taste and add more oil if necessary.

Serves 4–6

NUTRIENT ANALYSIS PER SERVING 163 cal – 680 kJ – 12 g protein – 17 g carbohydrate – 11 g sugars – 6 g fat – 1 g saturates – 7 g fiber – 0.3 g sodium

HEALTHY TIP This dish is nourishing and excellent for those on a diet. It is rich in B1, B2, and B6 vitamins, potassium, sulfur, magnesium, and silicon. It also contains vitamin K.

Eggplant and tomatoes

This simple and healthy salad is known as *Zaalouk* in Morocco. I have steamed the eggplant, which helps to retain nutrients (although it is usually boiled or fried, which I prefer), but grilling is also a good option.

INGREDIENTS *1 lb eggplants, sliced into medium pieces* ‖ *3 garlic cloves, unpeeled* ‖ *½ tablespoon lemon juice* ‖ *8 oz tomatoes, peeled, seeded, and cubed* ‖ *2 tablespoons extra virgin olive oil, divided* ‖ *1 teaspoon salt, or to taste* ‖ *½ teaspoon paprika* ‖ *¾ teaspoon ground cumin* ‖ *2 tablespoons finely chopped cilantro leaves*

ONE Steam the eggplant and garlic. When the eggplant pieces are soft, transfer to a large dish. Peel the garlic, add to the eggplant with the lemon juice, and gently mash together. **TWO** Put the tomatoes and 1 tablespoon of the oil in a medium skillet. Sprinkle with the salt and simmer over medium-low heat, stirring occasionally. **THREE** When nearly all the water has evaporated, stir in the eggplant, paprika, cumin, cilantro, and remaining oil. Stir well for 1–2 minutes, taste and adjust the seasonings, and serve warm or at room temperature.

Serves 4

NUTRIENT ANALYSIS PER SERVING 80 cal – 339 kJ – 2 g protein – 5 g carbohydrate – 4 g sugars – 6 g fat – 1 g saturates – 4 g fiber – 0.5 g sodium

HEALTHY TIP This is an excellent salad with good levels of sulfur, magnesium, phosphorus, the antioxidant lycopene, selenium, and germanium, which relieves pain and detoxifies.

Couscous with milk and walnuts

Here is a quick and easy couscous dish. Moroccan people like to eat couscous with milk as a light, comforting meal in the evening.

INGREDIENTS *1½ cups organic couscous ‖ ½ teaspoon salt ‖ ⅓–½ cup walnuts, finely ground ‖ 1 teaspoon turmeric ‖ ¼ teaspoon ground cinnamon ‖ small pinch dried lavender (optional) ‖ 1 cup 2 percent milk ‖ 1 bay leaf ‖ 1 cinnamon stick ‖ ½ tablespoon honey ‖ ½ teaspoon orange flower water or rosewater (optional) ‖ 4–5 dates, preferably medjool, cubed or coarsely chopped*

ONE Cover the couscous with water. Rake it through with your fingers, then drain and immediately spread it evenly over a large tray or shallow pan. Rake the grains with your fingers a few times to aerate them, then leave for 20–30 minutes until the water is absorbed and the couscous is relatively dry. **TWO** When dry, rub the couscous gently between your palms, allowing it to fall back into the tray or pan, to break down any lumps. Repeat until all the couscous has no lumps. Sprinkle the couscous with the salt, walnuts, turmeric, ground cinnamon, and lavender, if using, and mix thoroughly. **THREE** Put the milk, bay leaf, and cinnamon stick in a large pan and bring to a boil. Add the honey and stir until dissolved. Add the flower water or rosewater, if using, remove the bay leaf and cinnamon stick, and remove from heat. **FOUR** Add the couscous to the hot milk, stir, cover, and leave until the milk has been absorbed. **FIVE** Transfer to a serving dish and mix in the dates, using a fork. Serve warm or at room temperature.

Serves 4

NUTRIENT ANALYSIS PER SERVING 423 cal – 1723 kJ – 10 g protein – 53 g carbohydrate – 14 g sugars – 19 g fat – 2 g saturates – 2 g fiber – 0.3 g sodium

HEALTHY TIP This salad supplies the body with nutrients and minerals important for the proper function of the brain and nervous system. It is rich in omega-3 fatty acids, which protect the heart, and vitamins E and B, as well as calcium, magnesium, copper, phosphorus, boron, and magnesium. The turmeric adds more benefits that may protect the body and liver against cancer and toxins.

Couscous with seven vegetables This is the national dish of Morocco.

INGREDIENTS *½ cup dried chickpeas, soaked overnight* ‖ *1 lb boneless lamb (leg or shoulder)* ‖ *7½ cups water* ‖ *2 bay leaves* ‖ *2 cinnamon sticks* ‖ *5 small onions, about 1 lb, peeled and cut into 6 pieces* ‖ *good pinch saffron threads* ‖ *1 teaspoon ground ginger, divided* ‖ *1½ tablespoons extra virgin olive oil, divided* ‖ *3–4 cilantro sprigs* ‖ *3–4 parsley sprigs* ‖ *½ small white cabbage, cut into 3 pieces* ‖ *4 small carrots* ‖ *1 turnip, quartered* ‖ *1 eggplant, about 8 oz* ‖ *4 medium pieces pumpkin, peeled and seeded* ‖ *4 baby zucchini* ‖ *3 tomatoes, halved* ‖ *2½ teaspoons salt, divided, or to taste* ‖ *¾ teaspoon black pepper* ‖ *good pinch turmeric* ‖ *¾–1 teaspoon paprika* ‖ *1¾ cups organic couscous*

ONE Put the drained, rinsed chickpeas in the bottom of a couscoussière or pan with the lamb, water, bay leaves, and cinnamon sticks. Bring slowly to a boil, skimming the surface. Cover and simmer for 5 minutes, reduce heat to low and simmer for another 40 minutes. **TWO** Add the onions, saffron, ½ teaspoon of the ginger, ½ tablespoon of the oil, the cilantro, and parsley, cover and cook 15 minutes. Add the cabbage, carrots, and turnip and cook 10 minutes. **THREE** Meanwhile, cut the eggplant lengthwise into quarters to within ½ inch of the stem, leaving it attached at the end. Add to the pan with the pumpkin, zucchini, and tomatoes. Add 1¼ teaspoons of the salt, the remaining ginger, the pepper, turmeric, and paprika. Simmer 10–15 minutes or until the meat and vegetables are tender. **FOUR** Meanwhile, cover the couscous with water. Rake it through with your fingers, then drain and immediately spread it evenly over a large tray or shallow pan. Rake the grains with your fingers a few times to aerate them, then leave for 20–30 minutes until the water is absorbed and the couscous is relatively dry. **FIVE** Rub gently between your palms, allowing it to fall back into the tray or pan, to break down any lumps. Steam in the top of the couscoussière or strainer for 20–30 minutes. **SIX** Remove and spread over a large tray, sprinkle with water and the remaining salt and aerate and separate the grains as before. Leave until the water is fully absorbed and gently rub again. Steam for a further 20–30 minutes. **SEVEN** Remove and spread over a large tray, sprinkle with the remaining oil and 1–2 ladles of stock and stir gently with a fork. **EIGHT** Discard bay leaves and cinnamon sticks. Serve topped with the vegetables and meat.

Serves 4–6

NUTRIENT ANALYSIS PER SERVING 676 cal – 2834 kJ – 44 g protein – 90 g carbohydrate – 23 g sugars – 18 g fat – 6 g saturates – 13 g fiber – 1.1 g sodium (if using 2 teaspoons salt)

HEALTHY TIP This dish is an excellent source of protein, antioxidants, fiber, and valuable amounts of B vitamins.

Pastries

Briouats with vegetables

In Morocco, briouats, as a general rule, are served as starters along with salads. They're invariably filled and are packed with good nutrients. Here, they are filled with a mixture of colorful vegetables—the pastry disguise might attract children to eat some. They are excellent to serve at parties, since they can be prepared ahead of time.

INGREDIENTS *1 tablespoon extra virgin olive oil* ‖ *1 teaspoon clarified butter (see page 14)* ‖ *7 oz turnip, coarsely grated* ‖ *7 oz carrots, coarsely grated* ‖ *7 oz zucchini, coarsely grated* ‖ *1 teaspoon salt* ‖ *½ teaspoon turmeric (optional)* ‖ *1 teaspoon black pepper* ‖ *4 sheets filo pastry, or as necessary* ‖ *1 egg yolk, beaten* ‖ *peanut oil, for brushing* ‖ *chopped mint, to garnish*

ONE Heat a skillet, add the oil and butter, and heat until melted. Add the vegetables and cook for 8 minutes or until they reduce in size. Season with the salt, turmeric (if using), and pepper. Remove from heat and let cool. **TWO** Meanwhile, fold the filo sheets in half and, using scissors, cut strips of 2½ inch widths. Keep the sheets you're not using under a wet cloth. Take 1 heaping teaspoon of the vegetable mixture and place it in the corner at the narrow end of one filo strip. Fold this corner up and over on the diagonal to make a triangle shape, then keep folding, left then right, until there is just one fold to go. Moisten the end of the filo with beaten egg yolk, make the last fold, and gently press on the triangle to seal. Repeat with the remaining filling and filo. **THREE** Brush lightly all over with oil, place on a baking sheet, and bake in a preheated oven, 350°F, for 15 minutes or until golden. Serve with a sprinkling of chopped mint leaves.

Makes 16–18

NUTRIENT ANALYSIS PER SERVING 50 cal – 1214 kJ – 1 g protein – 7 g carbohydrate – 2 g sugars – 2 g fat – 1 g saturates – 1 g fiber – 0.2 g sodium

HEALTHY TIP These briouats are nutritious, rich in betacarotene, potassium, niacin, and calcium. They contain little saturated fat.

Briouats with meat

These irresistible triangles are to die for—as you bite into one, you will want to have more and more. Briouats are easy to make and freeze well to be reheated when needed.

INGREDIENTS *1 tablespoon extra virgin olive oil‖ 1 small onion, finely chopped‖ 1 red bell pepper, about 5 oz, cored, seeded, and finely chopped‖ 1 green bell pepper, about 5 oz, cored, seeded, and finely chopped‖ 1 teaspoon ground cumin ‖ ¾ teaspoon paprika‖ ¼ teaspoon black pepper‖ 8 oz ground lamb‖ ¾ teaspoon salt‖ 3 heaping tablespoons finely chopped cilantro leaves‖ 3 heaping tablespoons finely chopped parsley‖ 5 sheets filo pastry, or as needed‖ 1 egg yolk, beaten‖ peanut oil, for brushing*

ONE Heat a fairly large skillet. Add the oil, onions, and chopped peppers and cook, stirring occasionally, for 3–5 minutes. Season with the cumin, paprika, and pepper and stir well, then add the lamb and salt and cook the meat for 3–4 minutes, stirring, to brown thoroughly. Continue to cook, stirring occasionally, until any liquid has almost evaporated but it has not dried out. Just before the end of cooking time, stir in the cilantro and parsley. **TWO** Fold the filo sheets in half and, using scissors, cut strips 2½ inches wide. Keep the sheets you're not using under a wet cloth. Take 1 heaping teaspoon of the meat mixture and place in the corner at the narrow end of one filo strip. Fold this corner up and over on the diagonal to make a triangle shape, then keep folding, left then right, until there is just one fold to go. Moisten the end of the filo with beaten egg yolk, make the last fold, and gently press on the triangle to seal. Repeat with the remaining filling and filo. **THREE** Brush lightly all over with oil, place on a baking sheet, and bake in a preheated oven, 350°F, for 15–20 minutes or until golden.

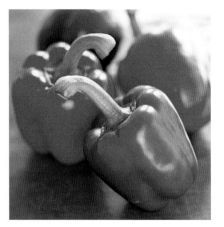

Makes 24

NUTRIENT ANALYSIS PER SERVING 53 cal – 220 kJ – 3 g protein – 5 g carbohydrate – 1 g sugars – 2 g fat – 1 g saturates – 0 g fiber – 0.2 g sodium

HEALTHY TIP These briouats are rich in protein, betacarotene, vitamin C, phosphorus, magnesium, and iron.

Briouats with goat cheese

These briouats enclose a mixture of goat cheese and parsley and would be good to serve at any occasion, even at a picnic. Briouats are made with many interesting fillings, so experiment with your own ideas. For instance, for this recipe, try adding some pitted and chopped black olives, and use mint instead of parsley.

INGREDIENTS *5 oz soft goat cheese* ‖ *4 heaping tablespoons finely chopped parsley* ‖ *pinch black pepper* ‖ *pinch salt, if necessary* ‖ *2 sheets filo pastry, or as needed* ‖ *1 egg yolk, beaten* ‖ *peanut oil, for brushing*

ONE Mix the cheese, parsley, and pepper together thoroughly. Taste the cheese mixture and if necessary add the salt. **TWO** Slice the filo sheets into strips of 2½ inches wide. Keep the sheets you're not using under a wet cloth. Take 1 tablespoon of the cheese mixture and place in the corner at the narrow end of one filo strip. Fold this corner up and over on the diagonal to make a triangle shape, then keep folding, left then right, until there is just one fold to go. Moisten the end of the filo with beaten egg yolk, make the last fold, and gently press on the triangle to seal. Repeat with the remaining filling and filo. **THREE** Brush lightly all over with oil, place on a baking sheet, and bake in a preheated oven, 350°F, for 15 minutes or until deep golden.

Makes 14

NUTRIENT ANALYSIS PER SERVING 45 cal – 188 kJ – 2 g protein – 3 g carbohydrate – 0 g sugars – 3 g fat – 1 g saturates – 0 g fiber – 0.07 g sodium

HEALTHY TIP These are delicious and healthy and good for children or menopausal women, since they contain calcium, important for strong bones, teeth, and heart muscles. In addition, they contain vitamins K and B, calcium, phosphorus, and protein.

Briouats with shrimp and sea bass

For non-lovers of fish, this may be an excellent way to include it in the diet. The shrimp and sea bass are steamed for a short time, then combined with olive oil, lemon juice, cilantro, and cumin. Briouats are very versatile, as they can be filled with any seafood, such as angler fish, lobster, salmon, or tuna, or with meat, fruit, or nuts.

INGREDIENTS *2½ cups water* ‖ *1 parsley sprig* ‖ *1 slice lemon* ‖ *1 bay leaf* ‖ *12 large raw shrimp, peeled* ‖ *10 oz sea bass fillets* ‖ *1–1½ tablespoons extra virgin olive oil* ‖ *¾ teaspoon ground cumin* ‖ *handful finely chopped cilantro leaves* ‖ *3 tablespoons lemon juice, or to taste* ‖ *1 teaspoon salt* ‖ *about ¼ teaspoon black pepper* ‖ *3 sheets filo pastry, or as necessary* ‖ *1 egg yolk, beaten* ‖ *peanut oil, for brushing*

ONE Put the water, parsley, lemon, and bay leaf in the bottom half of a couscoussière or pan and bring to a boil. Put the shrimp and sea bass into the perforated top section, or a steamer, and steam for 3–4 minutes, then remove and let cool. Chop the shrimp and fish into medium-sized pieces. **TWO** Heat the oil in a skillet, then add the chopped shrimp and fish, the cumin, and cilantro and cook, stirring, for a few seconds. Add the lemon juice, salt, and pepper, remove from heat, and let cool. **THREE** Fold the filo sheets in half and, using scissors, cut strips 2½ inches wide. Keep the sheets you're not using under a wet cloth. Take 1 heaping teaspoon of the fish mixture and place in the corner at the narrow end of one filo strip. Fold this corner up and over on the diagonal to make a triangle shape, then keep folding, left then right, until there is just one fold to go. Moisten the end of the filo with beaten egg yolk, make the last fold, and gently press on the triangle to seal. Repeat with the remaining filling and filo. **FOUR** Brush lightly all over with oil, place on a baking sheet, and bake in a preheated oven, 350°F, for 15 minutes or until deep golden.

Makes about 21

NUTRIENT ANALYSIS PER SERVING 47 cal – 198 kJ – 4 g protein – 3 g carbohydrate – 0 g sugars – 2 g fat – 0 g saturates – 0 g fiber – 0.2 g sodium

HEALTHY TIP These briouats are very nutritious, supplying zinc, vitamin E, and omega-3 fatty acids, which are important for the normal function of the immune system, and more so for men, who lose zinc. Olive oil is rich in vitamin E.

Desserts

Gazelle's horns

This Moroccan sweetmeat is one of the most refined, and long ago it was eaten at private celebrations of the wealthy. In Arabic it's called *Kaab al-ghazal*, which literally means "gazelle's heel." The French, on the other hand, called it *Cornes de Gazelle*. I believe that the Arabic title is correct because the shape stands up and curls around like a gazelle's heel. Here, I opted to cover the paste with sesame seeds. Sugar can be omitted and then the sweet can be dipped in a little honey after being baked.

INGREDIENTS ½ cup almonds, with skins on ‖ ½ cup blanched almonds ‖ 1 teaspoon peanut oil or clarified butter (see page 14), plus oil for greasing ‖ 2 teaspoons orange flower water ‖ pinch black pepper ‖ 2 teaspoons confectioners' sugar ‖ 1 teaspoon honey ‖ pinch ground cinnamon ‖ pinch ground ginger ‖ small pinch ground cloves ‖ 1 egg white ‖ 4 heaping tablespoons sesame seeds, or as needed

ONE Put all the almonds in a food processor and blend to a smooth consistency. Turn out into a bowl and add the oil or butter, flower water, pepper, confectioners' sugar, honey, cinnamon, ginger, and cloves and knead to mix thoroughly. If it's not malleable enough, add a little water. **TWO** Divide the mixture into 10 pieces, roll each piece into a small sausage, and then into a crescent shape. **THREE** Beat the egg white and lightly brush a baking sheet with oil. Roll each crescent in the egg white, then in the sesame seeds, and place on the baking sheet. Bake in a preheated oven, 350°F, for 10–15 minutes or until browned. **FOUR** Remove from oven and let cool.

Makes 10

NUTRIENT ANALYSIS PER SERVING 164 cal – 678 kJ – 6 g protein – 3 g carbohydrate – 3 g sugars – 15 g fat – 1 g saturates – 3 g fiber – 0.01 g sodium

HEALTHY TIP This is the kind of dessert that one can eat without any feelings of guilt. It is loaded with nutrients, such as vitamins E and B, calcium, magnesium, selenium, manganese, iron, and zinc, that protect against premature aging and cardiovascular and other diseases.

Briouats with rice

These reliable briouats are wonderful to work with and eat. Preparing them is quite therapeutic. I deviated from authenticity here and used brown rice instead of white because it is superior in nutrients and taste.

INGREDIENTS *⅓ cup brown rice* ‖ *⅔ cup water* ‖ *1¼ teaspoons salt, divided* ‖ *⅔ cup 2 percent milk* ‖ *1 cinnamon stick* ‖ *1 tablespoon clarified butter (see page 14)* ‖ *3½ tablespoons fructose (fruit sugar), divided* ‖ *10–12 blanched almonds* ‖ *1 teaspoon peanut oil , plus extra for brushing* ‖ *½ tablespoon orange flower water* ‖ *½ tablespoon rosewater* ‖ *2–3 sheets filo pastry, or as needed* ‖ *1 egg yolk, beaten*

ONE Put the rice, water, and salt in a small pan, place over low heat (if need be, put a heat diffuser under the pan), and simmer for about 15 minutes until the water is absorbed and the rice is soft. **TWO** Meanwhile, heat the milk with the cinnamon stick, butter, and 3 tablespoons of the fructose and stir to dissolve. Once the rice has absorbed all of the water, gradually add the milk, stirring continuously, and discard the cinnamon stick. Simmer until the milk has been absorbed and the rice is still moist. Remove from heat and let cool. **THREE** Put the almonds on a baking sheet and toast in a preheated oven, 350°F, for about 10 minutes. Remove from oven, place in a pan, and sprinkle with the remaining fructose, then leave for 1–2 minutes to caramelize. Brush a clean surface with oil, spread the caramelized almonds onto it, and let cool. Once cooled, chop coarsely and stir into the cooled rice with the flower water and rosewater. **FOUR** Meanwhile, fold the filo sheets in half and, using scissors, cut strips of 2½ inches wide. Keep the sheets you're not using under a wet cloth. Take 1 heaping teaspoon of the rice mixture and place in the corner at the narrow end of one filo strip. Fold this corner up and over on the diagonal to make a triangle shape, then keep folding, left then right, until there is just one fold to go. Moisten the end of the filo with beaten egg yolk, make the last fold, and gently press on the triangle to seal. Repeat with the remaining filling and filo. **FIVE** Brush lightly all over with oil, place on a baking sheet, and bake in a preheated oven, 350°F, for 15 minutes or until golden.

Makes 16

NUTRIENT ANALYSIS PER SERVING 66 cal – 276 kJ – 1 g protein – 9 g carbohydrate – 3 g sugars – 3 g fat – 1 g saturates – 0 g fiber – 0.06 g sodium

HEALTHY TIP These briouats are high in B vitamins and fiber, which help reduce the risk of diabetes. They also contain a good amount of magnesium, phosphorus, vitamin E, and calcium, which all contribute to combating diseases and aging. So you don't have to feel guilty about eating them—they give pleasure, an emotion that protects the heart and brain.

Orange confiture

You can't visit Marrakech or any other city in Morocco and not be tempted to prepare an orange or clementine confiture, since the fruits are cultivated there and you see them everywhere. So when oranges are in season, are juicy, and have a beautiful orange color, prepare this confiture. This is delicious on its own, with Rice Milk Pudding (*see page 151*), Rice Pudding with Almonds (*see page 148*), in a fruit salad, or as a filling for a sponge cake. Use within 2–3 weeks.

INGREDIENTS *2 lb navel oranges, scrubbed* ‖ *9 oz fructose (fruit sugar), divided* ‖ *1¼ cups water* ‖ *2 teaspoons lemon juice, divided* ‖ *2–3 cloves*

ONE Bring a large pan of water to a boil, add the oranges, and boil rapidly for 1 minute. Using a slotted spoon, transfer the oranges to a bowl of ice water and let stand 10 minutes. **TWO** Cut the oranges into ½ inch slices. Do not remove the seeds. Put the orange slices in a large shallow pan in a single layer. If necessary, cut a few slices in small pieces to fit in the gaps. Remove from pan and set aside. **THREE** Put 7 oz of the fructose in the pan, cover with the measured water, and place over low heat, shaking the pan until the sugar dissolves. Bring to a boil and add 1 teaspoon of the lemon juice and the cloves, then place the orange slices, and orange pieces if necessary, in the pan in a single layer. Return to a boil, reduce heat to medium-low, and simmer for 10–15 minutes, until most of the water has evaporated. **FOUR** Sprinkle all over with the remaining fructose, shake the pan, increase the heat, and leave to caramelize on one side, then turn to color the other side. Turn the heat off. You should be left with about 2 tablespoons of the caramel sauce. **FIVE** Transfer the confiture to a bowl, cover with plastic wrap, and keep refrigerated for up to 3 weeks.

Makes about 2 lbs

NUTRIENT ANALYSIS FOR TOTAL QUANTITY 1344 cal – 5743 kJ – 8 g protein – 348 g carbohydrate – 348 g sugars – 1 g fat – 0 g saturates – 13 g fiber – 0.03 g sodium

HEALTHY TIP Orange confiture is rich in bioflavonoids, which protect capillaries.

Rice pudding with almonds

This is a succulent pudding, and it is very easy to prepare. A similar one is prepared all over the Levant and Middle Eastern countries, and may be the origin of this pudding. It is said that the Crusaders fell for its exotic aroma, so they brought its recipe back to England around the 16th century. The original recipe calls for soaking the almonds in milk, then pressing them to extract the almond milk, while here the pulp is also used.

INGREDIENTS *½ cup blanched almonds* ‖ *½–1 teaspoon extra virgin olive oil* ‖ *½ teaspoon confectioners' sugar* ‖ *⅓ cup ground rice* ‖ *2½ cups 2 percent milk* ‖ *5 tablespoons fructose (fruit sugar)* ‖ *¼–½ teaspoon mastic (gum arabic), ground with a little confectioners' sugar, or a little vanilla extract* ‖ *1–1¼ tablespoons orange flower water*

ONE Blend two-thirds of the almonds in a food processor until smooth and powder-like. **TWO** Heat the oil in a small skillet and sauté the remaining whole almonds over low heat, stirring occasionally, until golden brown. Remove and sprinkle with confectioners' sugar, then let cool and chop coarsely. **THREE** Put the rice and ground almonds in a pan and gradually whisk in the milk. Place the pan over medium heat and bring to a boil, stirring continuously with a wooden spoon. Keep stirring and add the fructose. Once the sugar has dissolved, add the mastic or vanilla and the flower water and stir for 1–2 minutes or until it thickens. Pour into a serving dish and spread evenly, then let cool. **FOUR** Decorate all over with the reserved chopped almonds and chill before serving.

Serves 6–8

NUTRIENT ANALYSIS PER SERVING 217 cal – 909 kJ – 7 g protein – 28 g carbohydrate – 17 g sugars – 9 g fat – 2 g saturates – 2 g fiber – 0.06 g sodium

HEALTHY TIP Rice pudding is healthy and light on the stomach. The milk and almonds ensure that it is highly rich in calcium, an essential mineral for building strong bones and teeth, and for maintaining and reducing blood pressure. It also benefits premenopausal women. This lovely pudding provides valuable amounts of vitamins A, D, and E, as well as phosphorus, magnesium, and potassium. Fructose is used instead of normal sugar because it releases less insulin.

Milk b'steeya

Here is a lovely mélange of crispy pastry and milk pudding. This authentic dish uses various fruit and nuts for flavor and nutrients; it is far healthier than cakes high in hydrogenated fats, sugar, salt, and additives.

INGREDIENTS *3 sheets filo pastry* ‖ *1 small egg yolk, beaten* ‖ *½–1 tablespoon extra virgin olive oil* ‖ *2 tablespoons ground rice* ‖ *generous 1⅓ cups 2 percent or skim milk* ‖ *finely grated rind of 1 orange (optional)* ‖ *½–1 tablespoon honey, or 2 teaspoons fructose (fruit sugar), or to taste* ‖ *1–2 bananas, thinly sliced* ‖ *¼ cup walnuts, coarsely chopped* ‖ *6 strawberries, thinly sliced* ‖ *1 mango, thinly sliced* ‖ *¼ cup blanched almonds, browned and chopped medium-fine* ‖ *a few mint leaves, chopped (optional)* ‖ *2 tablespoons hazelnuts, browned, chopped medium-fine (optional)* ‖ *⅓ cup pistachios, ground coarsely-fine (optional)* ‖ *¼–½ teaspoon confectioners' sugar*

ONE Fold each filo sheet 3 times to make a small square. Using a 4 inch diameter plate as a template, and with a pointed knife, cut around the pastry to form 8 rounds from each sheet. Lightly brush the center of one round with beaten egg yolk, cover with another round, gently press together, and brush all over with oil. Repeat with the remaining filo rounds. Place on a baking sheet and cook on the lower shelf of a preheated oven, 375°F, for 5–8 minutes until browned. Remove from oven and let cool. **TWO** Meanwhile, put the ground rice in a small pan and gradually add the milk, stirring continuously. Keep stirring until boiling, reduce heat, and simmer for 2–3 minutes, stirring occasionally (make sure that it doesn't burn). Stir in the orange rind, if using, remove from heat, and beat vigorously, then let cool. As it cools, stir in the honey or fructose. **THREE** To make one piece, place a filo round on a plate and spread with some banana and walnuts. (Alternatively, spread a thin layer of rice pudding under the banana slices.) Top with a second filo round and spread gently with a thick layer of the rice pudding. (If it breaks, don't worry, it won't show.) Spread the strawberries and mango over the rice pudding and sprinkle with almonds and some mint, if using. Cover with a third filo round, sprinkle with hazelnuts (if using), more almonds, and, if desired, some pistachios. Sprinkle with a little confectioners' sugar. Repeat with the remaining ingredients to make 3 more pieces and serve.

Serves 4

NUTRIENT ANALYSIS PER SERVING 544 cal – 2269 kJ – 15 g protein – 51 g carbohydrate – 26 g sugars – 32 g fat – 3 g saturates – 6 g fiber – 0.2 g sodium

HEALTHY TIP This dessert has valuable vitamins and minerals such as B, E, and C, potassium, calcium, and magnesium.

Rice milk pudding

This pudding was constantly prepared at my parents' house. The Moroccan version is very similar and evidently of an Arabic influence. It's easy to make and is a good way to increase the intake of calcium. When preparing this rice pudding, I like to use basmati rice for its lovely perfume. I add the milk gradually, but if preferred, add all the milk at once and stir from time to time. Very little sugar is used, giving you the opportunity to add some honey, jelly or marmalade. Another way of presenting it is with a coulis of strawberries or mangoes.

INGREDIENTS *1 cup white basmati rice, rinsed once and drained* ‖ *2½ cups water* ‖ *bouquet garni: 1 bay leaf, 1 cinnamon stick, 1 piece fresh ginger root, 1 cardamom pod* ‖ *pinch salt* ‖ *2½–3 cups 2 percent milk* ‖ *1½–2 tablespoons fructose (fruit sugar)* ‖ *¾–1 tablespoon orange flower water* ‖ *½ tablespoon butter*

ONE Combine the rice, water, bouquet garni, and salt in a medium pan. Bring to a boil, reduce heat to low, cover, and simmer for 10–15 minutes or until the water has been absorbed and the rice has softened but is still moist. **TWO** Remove the cinnamon stick. Add a little of the milk and stir every now and then until the rice absorbs the milk. Repeat until all the milk has been added and absorbed. Remove the ginger, cardamom, and bay leaf. Stir in the fructose, flower water, and butter. **THREE** Pour the milk and rice mixture into a blender or food processor and pulse briefly—it should be coarsely crushed, not puréed. Pour it back into the pan and heat for 2–3 minutes, stirring a few times. Transfer to a glass bowl and serve warm or chilled.

Serves 6–8

NUTRIENT ANALYSIS PER SERVING 185 cal – 777 kJ – 6 g protein – 35 g carbohydrate – 9 g sugars – 2 g fat – 1 g saturates – 1 g fiber – 0.06 g sodium

HEALTHY TIP This soothing dish is rich in protein, calcium, vitamin E, phosphorus, potassium, and magnesium. Milk may control high blood pressure and reduce the risk of osteoporosis, and this is a fabulous way to increase the consumption of milk—you'll see for yourself how enjoyable it is.

Dried fruit salad

While in Fez I was told that the first fruit *b'steeya* was prepared by a woman who worked at the Royal Palace for King Hassan to honor Margaret Thatcher, England's then prime minister. Here, dried fruits are simmered in water with various aromatic spices. Once cooled, they can be added to a seasonal fresh fruit salad with some chopped mint.

INGREDIENTS *¼ cup dried apricots* ‖ *¼ cup dried figs* ‖ *½ cup dried plums* ‖ *¼ cup raisins* ‖ *¼ cup sun-dried apples* ‖ *4–6 dried medjool dates* ‖ *bouquet garni: 1 cinnamon stick, 1 bay leaf, 2 cardamom pods, 1–2 cloves, 1 star anise* ‖ *2 tablespoons fructose (fruit sugar) (optional)* ‖ *1 teaspoon lemon juice* ‖ *pinch nutmeg* ‖ *pinch ground cinnamon* ‖ *good pinch freshly grated ginger root* ‖ *1 teaspoon orange flower water*

ONE Rinse the dried fruits well, drain, and place in a bowl. Cover with water and soak for 6 hours or overnight. **TWO** The following day, place the fruit and any remaining water in a pan with the bouquet garni and bring to a boil over medium-low heat. You may need to add a little water. Simmer for 10 minutes, remove the bouquet garni, and sprinkle with the fructose, if using, and the lemon juice, then simmer until the liquid has a slightly syrupy consistency. **THREE** Sprinkle with the nutmeg, cinnamon, ginger, and flower water and give it a good stir. Remove from heat and let cool. Serve as above.

Serves 6–8

NUTRIENT ANALYSIS PER SERVING 107 cal – 458 kJ – 2 g protein – 26 g carbohydrate – 26 g sugars – 0 g fat – 0 g saturates – 6 g fiber – 0.02 g sodium (Note: analysis does not include optional fructose.)

HEALTHY TIP This dish is very rich in betacarotene, E and B vitamins, iron, and magnesium.

Beghrir

These are crêpes, much loved by the Moroccans. They are eaten sprinkled with powdered sugar or bathed in honey. When a mother gives birth, it is customary to serve her crêpes for breakfast. Unsurprisingly, they're high in energy and very tasty. Here I use whole wheat flour, which is superior to white flour and has valuable amounts of the B vitamins, important for the proper function of the body's nervous system. On Sundays, after my morning run, I take one of these crêpes out of my refrigerator, brush its smooth side lightly with butter, and place under a hot broiler for a few seconds to crisp. I eat it with a little good-quality organic honey, a small piece of cheese, and whatever fruit is available, be it banana, mango, strawberries, papaya, or blueberries.

INGREDIENTS *½ teaspoon active dry yeast* ‖ *¾ teaspoon sugar* ‖ *⅔ cup whole wheat flour* ‖ *¼ cup all-purpose flour* ‖ *¾ cup water* ‖ *⅓ cup milk* ‖ *1 egg* ‖ *½ teaspoon whiskey (optional)* ‖ *peanut oil , for brushing*

ONE Dissolve the yeast in a small cup with the sugar and 2 teaspoons of warm water, cover, and leave in a warm place. **TWO** Sift the flours into a bowl, pushing as much bran as you can through the sieve, then tip any bran remaining in the sieve into the bowl. **THREE** Pour the water and milk into a small pan and heat to warm. Meanwhile, beat the egg and whiskey, if using, together in a small cup. Remove the milk mixture from the heat and, using a whisk, gradually whisk into the flours with the yeast and the beaten egg mixture. Beat well to aerate the batter, then cover with a thick cloth and set aside to rise in a warm place for 2 hours. **FOUR** Set a medium-small nonstick skillet over medium heat and brush lightly with oil. Whisk the batter again. When the pan is hot, pour a ladleful of the batter into the center. It will run to form a round crêpe. Cook for 20–30 seconds, or until the surface is dry, shaking the pan slightly. Transfer to a warm plate and repeat with the remaining batter, stirring the batter in the bowl every now and then. Grease the pan after every 2–3 crêpes using an oil-dampened piece of paper towel. **FIVE** Serve hot with honey, or as described above.

Serves 8

NUTRIENT ANALYSIS PER SERVING 78 cal – 326 kJ – 3 g protein – 9 g carbohydrate – 1 g sugars – 3 g fat – 1 g saturates – 1 g fiber – 0.02 g sodium (Note: analysis does not include optional whiskey.)

HEALTHY TIP This is a meal in itself, containing a wealth of vitamins, minerals, antioxidants, and protein, each of which has a role in maintaining a healthy mind and body, glowing skin, and shiny hair. This is excellent food for growing children, athletes, and the elderly. However, as good as it is, don't be greedy—try not to exceed a normal portion.

Ghoriba

These cookies are a little like shortbread—crunchy and smooth, with a velvety feel. The Moroccans prepare them in various ways—plain, using basic dough, or with nuts (mostly almonds), which they are very fond of. Their flavor is enhanced by aromatic spices, such as cinnamon or aniseed, and—for a stronger flavor—cloves. Personally, I love to use cardamom, which aids digestion. I was told by a Moroccan friend that almond and walnut *Ghoriba* are offered during important functions. They are good to enjoy with tea or coffee, but limit your intake to one or two, as they are high in sugar and saturated fat. When shaping the cookies, my advice is to let the dough crack of its own accord, so they look homemade, not store-bought.

INGREDIENTS *2–3 tablespoons clarified butter, melted (see page 14)* ‖ *3 tablespoons peanut oil* ‖ *1½ cup all-purpose flour* ‖ *5 tablespoons confectioners' sugar* ‖ *1 tablespoon orange flower water* ‖ *1 tablespoon water* ‖ *2 cardamom pods, seeds finely crushed in ¼ teaspoon confectioners' sugar* ‖ *⅓ cup coarsely chopped almonds*

ONE Pour the butter and oil into a bowl, sift in the flour, and stir in the confectioners' sugar, flower water, water, and ground cardamom. **TWO** Knead the mixture for 1–2 minutes in the bowl to form a dough, then turn it out onto a clean surface. At first it may be crumbly, but keep kneading, shape it into a ball, and place back in the bowl. Cover and let stand for about 30 minutes. **THREE** Remove the dough and knead again, then add the almonds and reform into a ball as before. Pinch off a little dough the size of a walnut and roll and press between your palms to form a round shape. As you press, it will naturally crack around its edges. Repeat with the remaining dough. **FOUR** Place on a baking sheet and cook in a preheated oven, 350°F, for 10–15 minutes. The base will brown and the surface will have a white cream color. Remove from oven, let cool, then serve with a sprinkling of confectioners' sugar.

Makes 10

NUTRIENT ANALYSIS PER SERVING 160 cal – 676 kJ – 2 g protein – 16 g carbohydrate – 5 g sugars – 10 g fat – 4 g saturates – 1 g fiber – 0 g sodium

HEALTHY TIP Don't feel guilty when eating this dessert, as it does contain nutrients that will help to beautify the skin, calm the nerves, feed the brain, and lift the spirit. So enjoy!

Index

Author acknowledgments

This book wouldn't have been realized without the help and encouragement of many
to whom I wish to express my immense gratitude and heartfelt thanks:

To Rosy Kindersley of Books for Cooks in London.

To my husband Nabil and my daughter Nour for her accurate remarks.

To my brother, Fouad Kanso.

To Professor Mohammed Mezzine and Laila Benkirane for their inspirational gift,
the book they have translated from Arabic to French "Fudalat al-khiwan"
fi Tayibat al-taâm wa al alwan.

To Professor Lahlou for his kindness, Abdelrafii Benjelloun chef lecturer, for his
great help.

To Omar Lebrar of Dar el–Ghalia.

Many thanks to Marise Bergel for her precious time and effort.

To the National Tourism of Morocco.

To Aziz Murii for his time.

To Royal Maroc Airways.

To Ahmed Nait of Travelink who with devotion made my journey through Morocco
most enjoyable.

To his team who guided me with great care: Siddik Assem, Said Lemri, and Hisham
in Fez.

My heartfelt thanks to Monsieur and Madame Sefraoui of the beautiful Riad Fez
for their warmth and sharing the secrets of their delicious cooking.

Many thanks to Christope Robin, Jocelyne Leb, and Fabrizio Ruspoli of
La Maison Arabe in Marrakech for his time sharing his insight about
Morocco, especially Tangier.

My immense thanks to Melle Boukraa.F in Rabat, and to the owners and staff of
Loulema Essaouria, Kasbah Farm, Sawadi Skouraa, Kasbah Asma Rissani, and
El-minzah Hotel in Tangier—I still remember their lovely puff pastry Pastilla.

To my agent Deborah Rogers for having my best interests at heart, and to
Hannah Westland.

To Suzanne Walsh.

To Diane Klat.

To Nicola Hill for her devotion in making this book, Alice Bowden, William
Reavell, Leigh Jones, Sunil Vijayaker, Liz Hippisley, and to all who worked
on it.

PICTURE ACKNOWLEDGMENTS All photography © Octopus Publishing Group Limited/William Reavell with the exception of the following: Octopus Publishing Group Limited/Gus Filgate 35, 40, 79, 85, 95, 103, 108, 123, 124, 155; Ian Alexander/Natural Patterns Website (http://easyweb.easynet.co.uk/ ~iany/index.htm) 3 background.

EXECUTIVE EDITOR Nicky Hill
PROJECT EDITOR Alice Bowden
EXECUTIVE ART EDITOR AND DESIGN Leigh Jones
SPECIAL PHOTOGRAPHY William Reavell
SENIOR PRODUCTION CONTROLLER Martin Croshaw
FOOD STYLIST Sunil Vijayaker